For Jackie Quillen,
with many thanks for your interest in TWM,
and best wishes always –
Ned Conquest,
3/16/99.

The Widow's Might

Three Plays

by

Ned Conquest

THE APOLLONIAN PRESS

Richmond, Va. Washington, D.C.

Apollonian Press Edition, December 1997

Printed and published in Richmond, Virginia
The United States of America

Library of Congress Catalog Number 97-71095

ISBN 0-9627485-3-6

To the memory of my old friend
and college classmate,

John Jacob Nachtrieb
(16 July 1931 – 11 September 1996),

who, in the 1952 production of *A Modern Romance*
by Princeton's Theatre Intime, created the
rôle of Senator Harvey Harcourt.

Omnia scire, non omnia exsequi.
–Tacitus, *Life of Julius Agricola*

The Widow's Might

Three Plays

INTRODUCTION

Does the written word owe a greater debt to literature or to life? "Write about what you know"– the advice most often given aspiring authors – generally means, "Write about what you have lived." But is writing, in fact, inspired more by reading than by experience? The answer I know not, but perhaps literature and life are not to be so easily distinguished.

The plot of *The Widow's Might* came to me in fits and starts from the days of my early childhood. It derives from an anonymous medieval ballad, "The Wife of Usher's Well." When I first read this little poem, I must have been eight or nine years old. It made scant impact at the time, but over the years something about it beckoned me back. I have read it so many times by now that it seems almost ingrained.

A second influence on me was a short-short story entitled "The Open Window" by Saki (the pen-name of Hugh Herbert Munro). This, too, I read for the first time as a child. Of all Saki's whimsical tales, "The Open Window" still remains my favorite. I wrote *The Widow's Might* originally as a short story which ended at the first-act curtain of the present play. Saki's tale – quite different from mine in mood and purpose – ends at almost the same juncture. His takes place in a quiet Edwardian country home, while mine is set (as is the present play) in a Virginia farmhouse of the 1860's. I feel, though, that I was not much more than *technically* moved by Saki. And I like to think we were both inspired by the same antique original – "The Wife of Usher's Well."

In any case, the last two acts of *The Widow's Might* are altogether my own. Neither Saki nor the old balladeer is to blame for my "resolution." Though not exactly an afterthought, these last two acts appeared as such in time. One evening I read my short story aloud to a group of friends. No one left before the end, and all assured me of their interest. In the course of that reading, I came to see the story itself — most of which stands in the form of dialogue — as really a one-act play. And I felt, too, I had hardly done my main character justice. In due course, then, the last two acts materialized. With them in hand I re-worked the short story to present its action dramatically. Thus did the Wife of Usher's Well extend her ancient might!

The two other plays included here, both "one-acters," hark back to my last two years in college. While at Princeton, I attended plays whenever books and budget would allow. During my junior year I saw, at McCarter Theatre there, a full-length play called *The Moon is Blue*. I forget who wrote it; but "lighter than air" it was, and it fairly flew! Its boy-meets-girl-mash-and-mate plot made me think I could write something "no whit heavier" myself. The result was "A Modern Romance."

On a dare I submitted it to Princeton's Theatre Intime during the then-annual one-act play contest for undergraduates. The three winning plays were to be produced, and "A Modern Romance" tied for third place. The other third-place winner required more than a single set. My play, which called for only one, was therefore scheduled for production.

The three plays, each with its own cast, were presented at the Intime one after another on the same bill. During the spring of 1952, they enjoyed a run of three successive nights. Needless to say, I attended all performances. Admission was free, and the small house (as I recall) was filled to capacity on each of the last two nights.

Friends and faculty members had generous words for "A Modern Romance." Some of these reached me indirectly. The late Professor Willard Thorp remarked to a colleague (who later told me), "It's Philip Barry come alive again!" And the then president of the Intime let me know that a local New Jersey theatrical group had requested a special performance of my play without the other two. Princeton, however, engaged in no post-season contests; and the Intime staged no off-campus productions. "A Modern Romance" left the boards after its third performance.

To ready the text for present printing, I changed some of its topical references. In 1952, when the play strutted and fretted its hour upon the stage, Harry Truman was president. In making changes, I stayed with a Democratic incumbent and updated the allusions only as far as Jimmy Carter. In any future production, of course, these references could be reworked. As comedies always are, "A Modern Romance" was better on stage than on the page. I include it, though, as a *jeu de jeunesse* of which I have none but happy memories.

The last play, "For They Shall See God," had a vastly different origin and fate. During the fall of my senior year I took a remarkable course given by Professor Albert M. Friend – "Art 401: The Northern Renaissance." Probably for all who took it, but most certainly for me, Art 401 was unforgettable. The course yielded (among other things) this strange, little one-act play. To me, its inspiration was as meaningful as the play itself. In hopes that it may prove so to others, I include a further reminiscence.

Art 401 was open only to seniors. To enroll in it, one had to sit for a personal interview with Professor Friend himself. That interview was only the first ordeal. I left it convinced (as I still am) that Professor Friend admitted me to his course out of sheer compassion for my ignorance.

The course, in effect, was a graduate seminar. It consisted of lectures and preceptorials (all given by the Professor) which dealt as much with philosophy and religion as with art. To my great regret, both then and now, I had had no formal training in philosophy. What little I knew of the subject came from literature courses and from outside reading. I believe only a handful of others in Art 401 shared my deprivation. With great good grace Professor Friend answered questions from the unenlightened (most often, me). Those questions must have galled him, but he never showed it. The course meanwhile went its intriguing way. We pored over portraits, statues, Last Judgments, cathedrals, altar pieces – and macabre manifestations of the late medieval preöccupation with death and its many "dances."

Toward the end of the course we were shown pictures of a most unusual statue – "René of Châlons" from Bar-le-Duc, France. It was sculpted as a funerary memorial to René, a soldier, who had asked before he died that he be depicted on his tomb as he would look *five years after his death*. The anonymous sculptor took René at his word. The statue is that of an erect, though decaying, corpse. What remains of one hand clutches a shield, which indicates the calling of its bearer. The bones of the other arm are raised to heaven, its stringy fingers holding up an object the size of an apple. This object, we learned, was the soldier's heart. The almost fleshless face is likewise turned to heaven. In spite of its decomposition the face holds a haunting expression of hope. Face and figure both bespeak a willingness to endure even the annihilation of death, if God will but accept the proffered heart. Themes of portraiture, *danse macabre*, Last Judgment – all came together in "René of Châlons." A viewer might be pardoned for passing judgment himself on any god who would not accept so abject an offering.

In addition to a final examination, Professor Friend required of all his students a "term paper." He promised to post its *subject* on his bulletin board two weeks before the due date. The subject, as thus at last announced, was: "To be, or not to be – that is the question." Instead of a paper, we were told, each student might submit a creative work of his own which, in terms of the course materials, dealt with the posted subject. In past years students had submitted paintings, music, sculpture, poems, short stories, novelettes. Occasionally some one had even written an essay. My own effort consisted of two sonnets and the one-act play, "For They Shall See God."

As an interview had been a prerequisite to enrollment, so an hour's private conference on one's "term paper" was required as a *coup de queue*, if not a *coup de grâce*. I went to that final conference in fear and trembling. Professor Friend floored me. He said he had liked the sonnets and the play, too. He even asked for a copy of all three to keep. "I am not worried," he told me, "about your understanding of the course: we can talk about anything you like." Job, when he heard that voice out of the whirlwind, could not have been stricken more perfectly dumb.

Professor Friend helped me. He said, "I see from your play that you are familiar with *The Green Pastures*." I did know – and love – Marc Connelly's play. During my freshman year I had seen its Broadway revival (directed by Connelly himself). This I could talk about! Needless to say, Professor Friend knew the play better than I did. He set me straight on aspects of it which had long troubled me. It was as if he and I were discussing a beloved mutual relative!

Having dealt with Connelly's play, the professor turned to mine. He asked whether I had actually known any one like my protagonist, Henry Hill. I said no, but that I remembered hearing of such a person. Listening to radio evangelists is not something I have often done, even during childhood; but at least once in my young life I had heard an "orator of the air" who impressed me. He preached about an actual man who had, in the early years of this century, undergone the bodily "penance" which Henry Hill endures in the play. No one had known of the man's condition until he died. As he had led an exemplary life, his friends were at a loss as to why he had chosen so to mortify his flesh. I forget what moral the evangelist drew from it all; the act itself I never forgot.

I mentioned to the professor another influence on me – Nathaniel Hawthorne's short story, "The Minister's Black

Veil." To have once read that story was, for me, to be haunted by it. Even so, I sometimes wondered, on re-reading it, whether the penance done by Father Hooper (Hawthorne's worthy divine) might not have been more effective had it remained a private act rather than one for all the world to see. (Even in the tale of Hester Prynne the infamous scarlet letter becomes at last a badge of all-too-human pride.) Of course, Father Hooper dons his veil at tremendous sacrifice: it effectively cuts him off from the warmth and geniality of human association. And he *is* a preacher intent on teaching his flock – which, by the end of the story, seems to encompass all of Massachusetts, if not New England. Henry Hill, though comparable in a way to Father Hooper, is not a minister: he feels himself altogether unworthy to preach. And his "penance," though voluntary, remains (to the world) unknown, or at best enigmatic. Perhaps moved by my own peculiar Protestantism, I tried to depict in Henry Hill a man whose first and last judgment is a matter between himself and God.

At the end of our talk Professor Friend suggested that I submit my play to the Theatre Intime for production. I did so, in the one-act play contest that spring. It failed even to place. The president of the Intime for that year told me the contest was for *producible* plays. Mine, he said – though he and other readers had liked it – would have been impossible to cast. Having missed its best opportunity, "For They Shall See God" never saw production.

Later that spring I happened to meet Professor Friend on the campus. We were both walking alone, I on my way to the library and he coming from it. Each of us carried an armful of books. He remembered me and spoke to me by name. During the brief conversation we had, he asked me whether I had shown my play to the Intime and, if so, how it had fared. With great regret I told him that the play had been refused production. He frowned and nodded: "That's like the Intime! They never produce anything but name-plays or just plain trash!" Apparently Professor Friend did not know the Intime had produced a play of mine the previous spring. (Or perhaps he *did*!) At any rate, *I* had never mentioned to him "A Modern Romance." I did not feel I should do so now. He cautioned me not to be discouraged, wished me well, and went his way. I went my own, to the library. Ever since, my little drama has slept the sleep of the all-unborn.

Such, then, is the background of the three plays here presented. All are about what I have known, though not (except in the imaginative sense) about what I have lived. Art and literary idols indeed are always with us. Like all others, even idols such as these are not to be worshipped and glorified. But (*Io, Apollo*!) may their influence be as ever beneficent as it is secure!

THE WIDOW'S MIGHT

A Play in Three Acts

THE CHARACTERS

MRS. BRADY, a widow in her late sixties

JUDY BARDEN, her companion, a girl of almost twenty

SERGEANT WADE
PRIVATE CHILTON
PRIVATE HARGREAVES — Troopers of the 10th Virginia Cavalry Regiment

MARTIN FERGUS, chaplain of the 10th Virginia

A VISITOR

THE WIDOW'S MIGHT

ACT I.

Scene: Parlor and front porch of THE WIDOW BRADY'S *house.*
Time: Twilight of 10 November 1862, an Indian summer evening in Northern Virginia. The stage darkens twice to denote the passage of time–in the first instance, a period of more than an hour; in the second, a period of several hours.

The curtain rises to reveal porch and parlor of the house. The front (or outside) wall of the house slants steeply forward from deepstage left to downstage left. In this wall the front door, deepstage left, opens from the hall of the house onto the front porch. The porch extends from deepstage left almost to the downstage edge of the outside wall. Two unadorned square columns support the roof of the porch. Steps lead down, far left, from the porch to the ground. In the outside house-wall, left, a large window, downstage of the hall and the front door, looks out across the porch to the driveway, which approaches the house from offstage left. The back wall of the parlor, parallel to the footlights, separates the parlor from the front hall behind it. In this wall a double doorway, left of center, leads from the parlor into the front hall. Behind this double doorway the back wall of the hall itself stands deepstage rear. The front door of the house, deepstage left, can just be seen through the double doorway to the parlor. The front hall contains stairs, off right, which lead to the second story, and doors, also off right, which lead to the kitchen and to other rooms on the first floor. Neither the stairs nor these doors to other rooms are visible.
The parlor is furnished simply. Against its rear wall, and right of the double doorway, stands a black horsehair sofa, some six feet in length. Downstage right of the sofa stands a table with,

on either side, a straight-backed chair facing into the room. Downstage left of the double doorway, and near the large front window, are two more straight-backed chairs with a small table between them. The upstage one of these two chairs is higher-backed and heavier than the other chairs in the room. It stands angled left to face the large front window. An inexpensive engraving hangs above the sofa.

When the curtain rises, MRS. BRADY *is seated comfortably in a wooden chair on the porch. She is more dignified than handsome. Her white hair is drawn severely back in a knot behind her head. She wears a long, high-necked dress of solid black, belted, with white lace at cuff and collar. She is gazing intently offstage left, down the driveway to her house.*

JUDY *is seated near her on the edge of the porch.* JUDY *is plain, though not unattractive. She has dark hair, worn like the older woman's, and a white blouse over a long skirt of dark green homespun. She, too, is staring off left, down the driveway. Oak and locust trees shade the drive and yard, left. Both women seem expectant.*

After a moment the beat of horse hooves, galloping, sounds off left in the distance. MRS. BRADY *sits forward at once, her hands gripping the arms of her chair.* JUDY *eyes her sharply, then turns back to the driveway.*

JUDY, *as she gazes off left:* Three soldiers – turning in at the gate. They're Confederate!

MRS. BRADY *half-rises, then drops back in her chair.*

MRS. BRADY: It's not *they*! – thought for a moment – !

JUDY, *slowly:* No. – No, *they* wouldn't be riding.

The beat of horse hooves, now walking, comes closer. The sound of a wagon is heard, off left.

MRS. BRADY *suddenly rises to her feet.* JUDY *leaps to the ground. Both stare hard, off left.*

JUDY: A wagon! – and there's a *body* in it!

MRS. BRADY: Wearing black, too. *That's* no soldier!

JUDY: You reckon they killed him?

MRS. BRADY: If he was a farmer, he wouldn't be the first. Yankees – ours, too, these days – they take what they want – and *kill*, if they think they have to.

Commands to "Hold up!" and "Dismount!" are heard, off left. Horses and wagon come to a halt. Three Confederate soldiers enter, left, and stand facing the porch. The foremost one of the soldiers has three stripes on his sleeve.

SGT. WADE, *removing his cap and addressing* MRS. BRADY: My respects, ma'am. I'm Sergeant Wade of the 10th Virginia. I saw your house, here by the crossroads, when I was out on a scout the other day. We're camped about a mile to the north. We just had a brush with Yankee cavalry yonder. *[Nods off to his right rear.]* Lieutenant Fergus – that's him, layin' out in the wagon – he caught a round through the chest. We were hopin' you'd be good enough to take him in, till he – till he gets over it.

MRS. BRADY *stares down at* SGT. WADE *but says nothing.* JUDY *watches her intently.*

SGT. WADE, *beginning to fidget:* The lieutenant's bad off, ma'am. He just caught a round –

MRS. BRADY, *cutting him off:* I'm not deaf, Sergeant! *[She glances over his head toward the wagon, off left.]* He's wearing black broadcloth, your "lieutenant." He doesn't look like a soldier to me.

SGT. WADE, *shrugging:* He's *not* a soldier, ma'am. He's a preacher – chaplain to the 10th Virginia. We just call him "Lieutenant."

FERGUS, *in a weak voice, off left:* 'S true. – I'm not a soldier.

MRS. BRADY, *walking to the edge of the porch: Are* you a preacher, then?

FERGUS, *still off left:* I am – though, God knows, you wouldn't be the first to think I'm not!

SGT. WADE, *his voice husky:* He's a damn' good one – if

you'll pardon my language, ma'am. All of us here can swear to that.

The two troopers behind him and the wagon-driver, off left, murmur inarticulate agreement.

MRS. BRADY: Bring him in.

SGT. WADE, *nodding and turning to the two troopers:* Chilton – Hargreaves! Be easy with him.

The two men go off, left, and return bearing the wounded chaplain. His black coat is bloodstained at the left shoulder. Heavy bandaging shows across his chest, under the coat.

MRS. BRADY *turns, opens the front door, and walks through into the parlor.* JUDY *goes with her.* SGT. WADE *follows; the men come after him with the chaplain.*

MRS. BRADY, *pointing:* You can put him on the sofa. It'll be cooler here in the daytime.

SGT. WADE: In the day – ? *[Stops suddenly.] Yes,* ma'am. In here, Chilton!

The men bring in the chaplain.

MRS. BRADY: Wait! – Judy! Go get the sheets off – off Robert's bed.

JUDY, *slowly:* Off – Robert's – ?

MRS. BRADY: *Yes,* girl. Be quick about it!

JUDY *darts out through the hall and up the stairs.* CHILTON *and* HARGREAVES *stand in silence, holding the chaplain.*

FERGUS, *weakly:* Haven't slept on a sheet in months. I won't miss it tonight. Don't strip your son's bed.

MRS. BRADY: How did you know he was my son?

FERGUS: If your husband were alive, he'd be with you – too old for this awful war. And the girl wears no ring.

MRS. BRADY: You don't miss much, for a punctured preacher.

FERGUS, *with a sad smile:* It's the much that won't be missing *me* I trouble about at the moment.

JUDY *re-enters with sheets and pillows. She makes a quick bed of the sofa.*

SGT. WADE, *to the men:* All right: lay him down – gentle.

They place the chaplain on the sofa, his head to stage right. JUDY *arranges the top sheet and blanket over his legs.*

FERGUS, *to the soldiers:* Thanks, men. I know you're tired – and you haven't complained.

SGT. WADE: They *better* not! *[Smiling.]* But none of us thought of complaining. God knows, it's the *least* we can do.

CHILTON, *nodding:* Sure as hell! *[Catches himself.]* I mean – I mean we'll make complaint to the Yankees.

HARGREAVES: You bet! Them *Yankees*'ll smart when we get *to* 'em.

SGT. WADE, *to the men:* See that they do! Now take on off. We've got to get back.

HARGREAVES *and* CHILTON *go out the front door, across the porch and off, left.*

SGT. WADE, *to the chaplain:* Goodbye, sir. We'll look in, soon as we get the time. *[To* MRS. BRADY.*]* Take care of him, ma'am. He's worth it.

SGT. WADE *exits, left, after the others. Sounds of the horses and wagon are heard fading away, left.*

MRS. BRADY *goes to the table, right, at the end of the sofa. She lights a candle on the table, then crosses to the tall chair, left, by the window. She sits in the chair and gazes out the window, down her drive.* JUDY *sits in the chair, right, at the end of the sofa.*

FERGUS: It's good of you to receive me, Mrs. – Mrs. – ?

MRS. BRADY, *without looking at him:* I'm Mrs. Brady. – It isn't "good" if it's a Christian duty, now, is it?

FERGUS, *after a pause:* But you know they brought me here to die?

Silence for a moment. As night comes on, the room and the yard outside begin to darken. MRS. BRADY *continues to sit with her eyes fixed on the drive.*

MRS. BRADY, *as she stares off, left:* I've been so much with my own dead that I'm not too good at telling just how alive *any* one is.

FERGUS, *after another pause:* Indeed – your husband. I hope not your son as well?

MRS. BRADY, *without looking at him: All* my sons – all three of them!

FERGUS: I'm sorry. – I'm sorry, too, that Sgt. Wade had to impose me on you.

The yard, left, begins to lighten faintly under moonlight.

MRS. BRADY, *not taking her eyes off the drive:* Think nothing of it. As well you as another.

Silence for a moment.

MRS. BRADY, *still not looking at him:* We've a little vegetable soup left from supper, if you're hungry.

FERGUS: Thank you, I couldn't eat. I'd be grateful for some water, though.

MRS. BRADY, *nodding toward the kitchen, right:* Judy!

JUDY *rises and goes out, right, through the hall. She returns shortly with a metal pitcher and a glass on a tray. She sets the tray on the table, right, and pours water into the glass. Supporting the chaplain's head, she holds the glass to his lips.*

FERGUS, *after swallowing:* Thank you. – Best water I've had since leaving home!

JUDY *sits again in her chair, right.*

MRS. BRADY, *not looking away from the drive:* We've got the finest well in four counties – cold – sweet – clear as ancient legend. One of the glories of the place – the *only* one at the moment.

FERGUS: A blessing, indeed. I should have said grace!

MRS. BRADY, *still not looking at him:* There *is* something stronger, if you feel the need.
FERGUS: Thank you. That wonderful water will do.
MRS. BRADY: Suit yourself.
Silence again. Outside, the yard grows darker. A sharp wind stirs the trees.
FERGUS: I fear I – I must make you both an apology.
MRS. BRADY *sits rock-still.* JUDY *looks at the chaplain.*
FERGUS: The men of the 10th Virginia, rightly or wrongly – and I'd be the first to say "wrongly," if they asked of *me*! – the men of the Tenth look on me as – as something of a hero. I've been there with them, the wounded – the *dying*, you know: so few ever recover! I've urged them to be brave – to trust in God – bear the pain and know they're going where pain itself shall die –! *[Pauses to catch his breath, then continues hoarsely.]* I've buried so many! – tried to comfort the others – writing letters – wrapping wounds, limbs, what's left of limbs. *[Pauses again.]* I rode with them when I could – walked behind them once when they went, dismounted, against some infantry. *[Coughs hard, wrenching his whole body.]*
JUDY *goes to him, puts the glass of water to his lips, and helps him drink.*
FERGUS, *as she settles him back:* Thanks! Thanks, child. *[His breaths come deeper and harder.]* It's just that I wanted to *do* something! I couldn't fight – kill – take life. I wanted to *save* life! – and all I've done is help so many to die!
MRS. BRADY, *still watching the drive:* If the men regarded you as a hero, *that's* something.
FERGUS, *perspiring heavily:* Well, their officers *think* they did. Our surgeon – Dr. Folton – he knows I'm not strong – knows, too, what it *means*, being shot through both lungs. Has no morphine, Folton – no, nor chloroform, either. After what he'd heard me tell the men – Sundays, and in that everlasting aid tent! – he didn't want them to see me go like a screaming child.

No, he told Sergeant Wade to "farm me out." (Thought I couldn't hear him, but I did.) Folton just – didn't trust me to make a "good death" of it, there with the rest. – Worst of it is – I'm afraid he was right!

MRS. BRADY, *her eyes on the drive:* No one knows what pain will do to him – or to her.

JUDY *rises and goes out, right, through the hall. She returns with a towel. Wetting one end of it from the pitcher, she bathes the chaplain's face.*

FERGUS, *his eyes closed:* Thank you.

MRS. BRADY, *as* JUDY *goes back to her chair:* Perhaps it's I who owe the apology. *[Turns to him, briefly.]* You see, Lieutenant – Reverend – (how do you like to be called?) –

FERGUS: I'd be glad if you called me "Martin."

MRS. BRADY: "Martin"?

FERGUS: It's my Christian name. In fact, tomorrow is my birthday – the Martinmass – Saint Martin's Day, you know. I was named for Saint Martin.

MRS. BRADY, *turning back to the drive:* Well, whomever you're named for, you've come to a house that has no saints about it. No, nor ever will. I left the church when my sons were taken from me. I'll go no more till I see the three of them home in flesh and blood – coming up that drive, just the way they went. I mean no slight to the sufferings of others. But I shed no tear for their pain: I have my own inside me, night and day. And each must bear his own: none can make *that* burden any lighter.

FERGUS: *God* can! Through time – through other human beings – God can.

MRS. BRADY, *waving her hand:* So I've heard. I've tried prayers and prayer meetings. Other people's tears just wear me out. A person lives and dies unto himself in this world. Physical pain may or may not be the worst of it.

FERGUS: But you've lost loved ones before. Your husband –

MRS. BRADY: Ah, my husband! Yes, he died twenty years ago – typhoid. I held him in my arms till he stopped shivering. (I knew he was gone then.) But he'd *had* his life – the best of it, anyway. And he left three sons behind. That was something. The three boys leave only me.

FERGUS, *glancing at the girl:* But your daughter –

MRS. BRADY: Judy is not my daughter.

JUDY: I would have been – if Jared – her youngest – had lived.

MRS. BRADY: She's here because she thinks I need looking after.

FERGUS: Who among us does not?

MRS. BRADY: I didn't ask it. Judy's my witness. She's free to go when she will.

FERGUS, *making himself smile:* Well, Judy – why *don't* you go?

JUDY, *slowly:* Because – if any one can bring him back, Mrs. Brady can.

Silence for a moment. The trees outside move now to a more insistent wind.

FERGUS, *shaken:* How – how can she bring him back?

MRS. BRADY, *eyeing the drive:* Go see that the fire's not out, girl. And bring my tea, if it's ready.

JUDY *goes out, right, through the hall to the kitchen.*

FERGUS, *quietly:* What have you told the girl?

MRS. BRADY: I've told her nothing. The girl sees what she sees.

FERGUS: And what does she see?

MRS. BRADY: She sees me sitting here, waiting – watching for them.

FERGUS: But *why*? – why are you watching?

MRS. BRADY: Because some day they'll come! They'll walk back up that drive just the way they once walked down it: Robert, carrying his father's great, old gun across one shoulder – Jared and Hiram, either side of him! – I want to be ready when they come. I don't know how long we'll have together.

Silence a moment.

FERGUS: Is this something you've prayed over?

MRS. BRADY, *sniffing impatiently:* What is prayer? A child's dream of toys on Christmas Eve!

FERGUS, *sighing:* Or the day before his birthday!

MRS. BRADY, *as if to herself:* Prayer never did a body harm – nor good, either, as I could see.

FERGUS: Prayer is communing with God. In its highest form it has no tangible goal.

MRS. BRADY: Communing with God, is it? What's so high about that? What's your God done for *you* of late?

FERGUS: Why, quite a lot! He's given me *you* to worry about instead of my own misery.

MRS. BRADY *laughs aloud. She turns from the dark outdoors and looks hard at the chaplain.*

MRS. BRADY: Well, you're not dead yet, Mr. Chaplain – Reverend – Martin! It'll take more than a Yankee bullet to do *you* in!

FERGUS: It'll do – a Yankee bullet.

JUDY *re-enters from the hall. She places a cup of tea in its saucer, on the table next to* MRS. BRADY.

MRS. BRADY, *tasting the tea:* Ah! *[Makes a face.]* You didn't give it time to brew!

MRS. BRADY *rises, takes the cup and saucer, and goes out through the hall to the kitchen. The chaplain glances at the girl.*

JUDY, *nodding toward the kitchen, as she sits again:* Very particular, that one. Always was.

FERGUS: What makes you think she can bring back her son?

JUDY: She can bring all three of 'em back.

FERGUS: How?

JUDY: She has ways. – I saw her bring a squirrel to life once. I found it dead in the garden.

FERGUS: How did she do it?

JUDY: Just held it in her lap – stroked it.

FERGUS: The squirrel may have been stunned – fell from a tree, perhaps.

JUDY, *shaking her head:* I don't think so.

FERGUS: Why didn't she bring back her husband?

JUDY: Because – she told you – she *saw* him go – felt him there, in her arms. She never saw her sons die.

FERGUS: But she speaks of them as being dead.

JUDY, *shaking her head again:* She doesn't believe it – not her!

FERGUS: Well, what happened to them?

JUDY: A letter came from Richmond – said they'd all been killed. Whole company lost – the one they were all three in. Happened on some hill or other – Malvern, I think it was. A whole company blown away! Of eighty odd men, there was only remains of twenty-four to *bury*! One big, common grave they got. Not even a stone to tell who's under it.

Silence. The girl glances out the window.

JUDY: Dead or not, I don't blame her for holding they'll be back.

FERGUS: Her faith that strong, is it?

JUDY, *staring out the window:* Not a matter of faith. She *knows.*

FERGUS, *after a pause:* Well, when are they coming?

JUDY: Maybe tonight – next month – a year from now. She'll bring 'em. They'll come to *her.*

The chaplain closes his eyes. He makes an effort to shift his weight and drops back, exhausted. MRS. BRADY *re-enters with cup and saucer. She places them on the table, left, and resumes her chair by the window. The chaplain makes another effort to move. He groans heavily.*

JUDY, *going to him and wiping his forehead again:* Can I do anything?

FERGUS, *breathing heavily:* Thank you! Thank you – not a thing!

Silence again. JUDY *returns to her chair. The wind outside grows stronger.*

FERGUS: You know, Mrs. Brady – there's a legend they tell, in the place where I was born. It involves the granting of a prayer to some one about to die.

MRS. BRADY, *once more staring out the window:* Oh? And what place is that?

FERGUS: Coleraine – in the north of Ireland. Do you know it?

MRS. BRADY: I do not. My husband was Irish. I'm not. I know nothing of Coleraine – and a sight less of its legends.

FERGUS: They say in Coleraine that, if a man has lived a good life – and if he dies on his own birthday – his saint (the one he's named for) may get the Lord to grant his final prayer. Of course, the man must know he's going to die – and the prayer has to be a worthy one. – And those with him at the time must join him in it. As Saint Chrysostom says, "when two or three are gathered together in thy name, thou wilt grant their requests." – Is this at all familiar, Mrs. Brady?

MRS. BRADY, *turning to look at him:* It is not.

FERGUS, *with a sad smile:* Of course, no one can know whether he's lived a good life or not. He may think he has – but the Lord, in his infinite wisdom, may hold the man mistaken.

JUDY: Well, what then of the prayer?

FERGUS: Why, then, the prayer would not be granted.

MRS. BRADY, *sharply:* You call this a "legend"?

FERGUS, *smiling faintly:* The people of Coleraine call it that! If the prayer fails, they hate to think it failed because their relative, or friend – the one who made the prayer – was an evil person. So they call it all a legend! Even so, few in Coleraine were ever willing to test themselves against it. (Few enough managed to die on their own birthdays!)

MRS. BRADY: It sounds like a legend to *me.*

FERGUS, *gently:* Well, of course, it does – to those who wish to think it such. But in defense of the good – or the apparently good – whose prayers went unanswered, the reason may have been that the object prayed for was an unworthy one.

MRS. BRADY: Can a "good" man, at such a time, pray for something unworthy?

FERGUS: Why, certainly! A good man can always sin, just as a sinner can sometimes do good.

Silence a moment.

FERGUS, *wearily:* The final prayer – well, it's rather like a last will and testament. Those with the dying man may seek improperly to influence his desires.

Silence again, as the chaplain catches his breath.

FERGUS: No doubt, it would be a great sin to do so – like forcing another to perjure himself to God. – The whole procedure! – fraught with traps for the unwary – *and* for the unfaithful!

MRS. BRADY, *sniffing impatiently:* The first you've mentioned of *faith.*

FERGUS: The dying man – if *he* have faith – will be heard. Those joining in his prayer must believe its object worthy – and know it to be attainable. They serve as a kind of testimonial – both to the perceived goodness of the one praying and to the goodness of his object. In Coleraine faith is taken for granted. Or so it used to be! The legend goes back to the Middle Ages.

MRS. BRADY: Have you known such prayers to be answered?

FERGUS: Not in recent years. But my parents brought me to Virginia as a babe in arms. The legend is part of my Coleraine heritage. In old books and parchments of the town one finds references to the granting of such prayers. In medieval times, it's said, the town was delivered of a terrible pestilence this way. In the eighteenth century such a "birthday prayer" ended a drought under which the entire county had suffered.

Silence again. The two women stare hard at the chaplain.

MRS. BRADY: And do you believe this – this legend of the "birthday prayer"?

FERGUS, *staring at the ceiling:* Had I not, would I have told you of it?

JUDY: When is the prayer granted – if it is?

FERGUS: On the day it's uttered, if at all.

MRS. BRADY: Why have you told us this?

The candle on the table, right, burns low and gutters. The wind outside rises.

FERGUS: Because I'd like to give *you* my last prayer. That is, I would like to pray with you – for what would seem to be your blessing.

MRS. BRADY: I'm not much on prayer.

JUDY: Nor am I.

FERGUS: *I'll* pray. But you must join – if only to say "Amen" when I'm done.

MRS. BRADY: If I like what I hear, I can manage that.

JUDY, *nodding:* I can say "Amen," if it pleases Mrs. Brady.

FERGUS, *looking hard at* JUDY: It had better please the *Lord!*

The candle sputters out. MRS. BRADY *rises and goes off, right, through the hall to fetch another. She comes back with it (already lighted), places it on the table, right, and sits again in her chair.*

FERGUS: I must say the prayer on my birthday – Martinmass – tomorrow – if I last till then! How much time do I have?

MRS. BRADY: Forty minutes. I looked at the hall clock when I fetched a light.

FERGUS, *softly:* I think – I can make it. *[Closes his eyes and appears to sleep.]*

The stage darkens to denote the passage of an hour or more. Suddenly, in the darkness, a guttural cough racks the chaplain. The stage lightens. The candle is seen to have burned quite low.

MRS. BRADY *is still sitting in her chair.* JUDY *kneels by the chaplain, bathing his cheeks and forehead with the damp towel.* MRS. BRADY *watches them intently.*

JUDY, *to the chaplain:* Are you all right? You scared us just then!

FERGUS, *weakly:* Yes – as all right as –

JUDY: Do you want to pray?

FERGUS, *dazed:* Pray?

JUDY: It's your birthday! *Has* been for some while.

FERGUS, *slowly:* Saint Martin's Day! – The day of my – ! *[Opens his eyes wide, straining to see.]* The legend! – Yes. – Are you both – both ready to join and – ?

MRS. BRADY: We are. *[*JUDY *nods as she kneels beside him.]*

FERGUS, *breathing hard:* Yes. – Well – I would like – very much – to pray.

The chaplain pauses a moment to gather strength and breath. With an effort he rouses himself on one elbow.

FERGUS: Merciful God! – and you, Saint Martin, whose name I bear – on this last day, which also was my first – I pray – that you restore her sons to this poor widow – whole and strong as when they left her. – And grant that he, the youngest, shall be forever hers who here awaits him. – In the name of the Father – Son – Holy Ghost – and through the blessing of Saint Martin, whose cloak is perfect charity! – Amen.

MRS. BRADY *and* JUDY *together:* Amen!

The chaplain falls back, exhausted. His breathing becomes more regular, though weaker. JUDY *resumes her chair.* MRS. BRADY *turns again to the window and the pitch-dark outdoors. A heavy rain begins to fall. Wind drives it against the house front. A strong gust rattles the window panes. The candle flickers out.*

Once again the stage becomes totally dark. The rainstorm gradually subsides.

Several hours pass.

Later, dawn slowly begins to break outside. The parlor lightens with the coming day. The chaplain is sleeping where he lies. MRS. BRADY *has slumped forward in her chair facing the window. In her own chair* JUDY *is sitting upright, wide awake. As dawn comes, she stares tensely through the window. A curling mist rises from the ground outside. All is quiet for a long moment.*

JUDY, *suddenly crying out:* Ahhh!

JUDY *leaps up from her chair. The chaplain stirs and opens his eyes.* MRS. BRADY *remains slumped forward, asleep.*

JUDY, *going to* MRS. BRADY *and shaking her:* There! I saw it! Through the mist – look! Coming up the drive –!

MRS. BRADY *jerks upright. She shakes her head, then rubs her eyes furiously.*

MRS. BRADY: What is it? What are you talking about?

JUDY, *moving around* MRS. BRADY'S *chair and pointing out the window:* There! – There! – They're coming! *[Her voice almost breaks.]* All of 'em – on foot! Robert in the middle with the gun on his shoulder! – Jared – behind him, to the right!

MRS. BRADY *follows her gaze and stares a moment. Then she leaps up so quickly that she knocks over the chair behind her. She presses herself against the window.*

MRS. BRADY, *hoarsely:* Good God alive! Hiram, too! – And Robert with the gun! Just like they left! – Good God alive!

The chaplain tries to raise himself. He has no strength. He presses his elbow against the back of the sofa.

FERGUS, *in a tortured whisper:* The pain! – God forgive me! *[Drops on the edge of the sofa, one arm dangling to the floor. He is dead.]*

The two women, their eyes fixed on the drive, never notice. Abruptly, MRS. BRADY *turns from the window. Shaking her head and muttering, she strides out through the hall to the front door, left.* JUDY *follows. The door is heard being flung back against the wall.* JUDY *steadies herself on the door frame and remains inside.* MRS. BRADY *steps out onto the porch. Hands on hips, she strains her eyes to see through the morning mist.*

MRS. BRADY: Why! – what's the matter with Hiram? – And that's not the way *Robert* used to walk! – God alive! It's not a rifle, either.

The sound of boots is heard on the muddy drive.

MRS. BRADY, *through tears, as she puts both fists up to her cheeks:* Come to me! Come – ! *[Shakes with silent sobs.]*

A muffled hysterical laugh is heard from JUDY, *who turns from the front door to hide her face.* MRS. BRADY *staggers back against the wall of the house.*

Three gray soldiers enter, left, through the mist. They stop and stand in line at the porch steps. On his shoulder the one in the middle carries a long-handled shovel. The one at the upstage end of the little line touches his cap and speaks.

SGT. WADE: Mornin' ma'am. Sergeant Wade, again. We moved up to the crossroads overnight. You wouldn't have heard us in the rain! You remember Chilton – him with the shovel – and Hargreaves, yonder beside him. Doc Folton *said* the Lieutenant wouldn't last till dawn. Thought you'd need a hand with the buryin', so we just walked over.

Curtain

ACT II.

Scene 1.

Scene: Parlor and front porch of THE WIDOW BRADY'S *house, as in* ACT I.
Time: Immediately after ACT I.

The curtain rises to reveal the same tableau that closed ACT I. MRS. BRADY *stands slumped against the front wall of the house, clenched fists at her cheeks, eyes staring.* JUDY, *at the front door, hides her face in her hands.* SGT. WADE, *upstage left, stands at the foot of the porch steps. Next to him is* PVT. CHILTON, *with the shovel on his shoulder.* PVT. HARGREAVES *stands downstage left, next to* CHILTON.

SGT. WADE, *after glancing at his companions:* I'm Sergeant Wade, ma'am. You remember *us* – Chilton –Hargreaves! We brought Lieutenant Fergus last night. Doc Folton told us he –

MRS. BRADY, *sharply:* I'm not deaf, Sergeant! *[More softly.]* I hear you! *[Lowers her hands and stands staring off beyond the soldiers, down the drive, left.]* God alive, I hear you!

JUDY *turns and comes out onto the porch. She approaches* MRS. BRADY *and takes her arm.* MRS. BRADY *shakes free without looking at her.*

JUDY, *softly:* It's Judy. – It's *Judy,* Mrs. Brady!

MRS. BRADY *nods, her eyes still fixed on the drive. Slowly she turns and walks back into the house. She stops at the sofa and stands, looking at the chaplain.* JUDY *follows and moves downstage right, her face in her hands. The soldiers stare at each other.* CHILTON *grounds his shovel and rests a boot on the blade.* MRS. BRADY *bends forward and touches the chaplain.*

MRS. BRADY, *calling to the men as she pulls herself up:* *Yes,* Sergeant! He – he must have – I mean, yes, he's dead! Come in.

SGT. WADE *glances at his men and nods toward the door.*

SGT. WADE, *as the men start up the porch steps:* Wipe your damn' feet! *[Scrapes his boots on the bottom step and enters the house.]*

CHILTON *and* HARGREAVES *kick at the bottom step and follow him into the parlor.* MRS. BRADY *moves right and stands by* JUDY, *who takes the older woman's hand in both her own.*

SGT. WADE, *after examining the chaplain:* Can you spare them sheets? If so, we'll wrap him in 'em.

MRS. BRADY, *nodding:* Take them!

SGT. WADE *pulls the top sheet up to cover the chaplain. He removes the blanket and lays it on the arm of the sofa.*

SGT. WADE: Where'bouts you want him? It'd be nice to put him where he won't ever be bothered.

MRS. BRADY: Yes. – Yes. Around back – down past the garden. There's a stand of trees –

SGT. WADE, *nodding:* Locust. I think I seen it when I passed this way the first time. Chilton – Hargreaves – get a holt of him. I'll bring the shovel. *[Takes the shovel, as the men turn to the sofa.]*

JUDY *buries her face in the older woman's shoulder.* MRS. BRADY *reaches up with her free hand to pat the girl's back.*

MRS. BRADY: Come, child. We'll show them.

Holding JUDY *close,* MRS. BRADY *moves with her across the room and out onto the porch.* SGT. WADE *goes behind them with the shovel. The men take up the body and follow. As the women descend the porch steps and walk, deepstage left, around the back of the house, the curtain falls.*

Scene 2.

Scene: The gravesite, a copse of locust trees at the foot of the widow's garden. No scenery. The action takes place downstage in front of the closed curtain.
Time: Immediately after Scene 1.

MRS. BRADY *and* JUDY, *who still clutches the older woman's hand, enter right and move to left of center stage, followed by* SGT. WADE *with the shovel. The two men, bearing the sheeted body, enter a few steps behind him.* SGT. WADE, *seeing the women stop, turns and motions, off right, to the men. They nod and move back, offstage right. The sound of the body being dropped to the ground jars the women apart. They turn to face* SGT. WADE.
SGT. WADE, *gesturing with the shovel:* About here all right?
MRS. BRADY *nods slightly. The sergeant makes the motions of scoring an outline in the earth. The men enter and stand, right, watching.*
SGT. WADE, *holding out the shovel:* Hargreaves! Take first go. It'll be the easiest. Rain last night softened the ground.
HARGREAVES *takes the shovel and (in pantomime) starts to dig where the grave is scored. All watch in silence for a while.*
SGT. WADE: Here! Lemme spell you, Hargreaves. I seen him dig the odd grave himself, the ol' lieutenant. *[Taking the shovel and working.]* He wasn't much good at it – not very strong, you know. But he tried. – Be a privilege to help with his.
HARGREAVES, *squinting up at the sun:* The way we're diggin', he'll be layin' north and south. That the way you want him?
SGT. WADE, *continuing to dig:* Good as any, I reckon.
HARGREAVES, *shoving his hair up under his cap:* 'Druther be east and west, myself – right with Mason and Dixon.

SGT. WADE, *as he digs:* Lieutenant Fergus wouldn't care. Hated this damned war. Just couldn't sit home and wait it out, he used to say.

CHILTON: Who the hell *could*, who's half a man?

All watch in silence as the sergeant continues to dig.

CHILTON, *to* MRS. BRADY: Ain't seen any menfolk hereabouts. Your husband with the army, ma'am?

MRS. BRADY, *still watching the sergeant:* With God's army, you might say. – My three sons –! *[She stiffens slightly.]* My three sons – they went with a regiment from the county. We got word they were all three killed at Malvern Hill.

CHILTON, *tipping his hat:* I'm sorry, ma'am. More than sorry!

MRS. BRADY, *still watching the sergeant:* So am I!

SGT. WADE: Well, Chilton, you a man and a half. So spell me!

CHILTON, *taking the shovel:* Glad to, Sergeant. *[Starts to dig.]*

SGT. WADE, to MRS. BRADY, *as he wipes his forehead:* Hot work, for men who were up all night!

MRS. BRADY, *to* JUDY: Go get the men some water, girl.

JUDY *goes off, right, past the men.* CHILTON *pauses a moment to glance after her.* HARGREAVES *watches her, too, as she goes. At a sign from* SGT. WADE, CHILTON *starts to dig again.*

MRS. BRADY: What do you know about him, Sergeant – this "lieutenant" of yours?

SGT. WADE: Not much, ma'am. 'Cept he was one hell of a preacher – if you'll excuse my sayin' it.

MRS. BRADY: I know that much.

SGT. WADE: Well, beyond that, I can't hardly say. Irish, I think he was – though he lived somewhere west of here – yonder, in the mountains. He never told us much about himself. 'Cept for when he preached or prayed, he was usually *listenin'*. You know how the men like to talk! – Or maybe you don't.

MRS. BRADY: I know how men like to talk.

SGT. WADE, *quietly:* I reckon you must, at that.

CHILTON *digs on in silence.* JUDY *returns, right, with a pitcher and a mug. She pours the mug full and offers it to* SGT. WADE. *He passes it to* CHILTON *first.*

CHILTON, *after drinking:* By God! That water's next best thing to whiskey!

HARGREAVES: Well, don't drink it all, yo' heathen hawg!

MRS. BRADY: There's plenty for all.

CHILTON, *to* HARGREAVES: Who you callin' a heathen hawg?

SGT. WADE, *taking the shovel and mug from* CHILTON *and passing them to* HARGREAVES: Wet yourself down, Hargreaves. And get on with it. Remember, the two of you: it's a man of the cloth you're buryin'.

HARGREAVES *takes a long drink.*

HARGREAVES, *wiping his mouth on his sleeve:* That's good stuff all right. Clear as country sky! Nary a varmint floatin' in it. *[To JUDY, as he begins to dig.]* Thank you, miss.

JUDY: You're welcome.

MRS. BRADY: We've got the best well for miles around. Been here since Washington's day.

CHILTON: Do it travel – that water?

MRS. BRADY: You can fill your canteens when you go.

CHILTON, *touching his hat brim:* Obliged to you, ma'am.

MRS. BRADY, *as if to herself:* The least I can do.

SGT. WADE *as he drinks the last of the water:* Keep on, men. He deserves a deep one.

HARGREAVES *grunts and nods as he continues to dig.*

MRS. BRADY: I'm thinking he was a deep one himself, your dead lieutenant.

SGT. WADE: You're right, ma'am. But I heard one of the

officers say it took education to know how deep he *was.* I couldn't keep up with all he told us. But it sure sounded good.

MRS. BRADY, *again as if to herself:* It didn't take much education for Judy and me.

SGT. WADE: He talked last night, did he?

MRS. BRADY: He talked.

SGT. WADE: Doc Folton said he wouldn't be good for much but screamin' till he died.

JUDY: He didn't scream. We didn't even know he was dead until *you* came.

HARGREAVES, *grinning to himself:* You sure he *is* dead?

CHILTON: If he wasn't, he'd be dead now, the way you dropped him.

HARGREAVES, *stopping: I* dropped him? Hell, *you* slung him down like he had a plague!

SGT. WADE: Just dig the damn' hole, Hargreaves.

HARGREAVES *goes back to digging.*

JUDY, *quietly:* No, I'm not sure he's dead.

HARGREAVES *stops again. The men look at each other.*

CHILTON: I seen him shot! You mean you think he's gonna get up and walk?

JUDY: He'll walk – whether he gets up or not.

SGT. WADE: What's your meaning, miss?

JUDY: I mean, I'll remember him.

SGT. WADE: So will I. *[Motions to HARGREAVES, who goes back to digging.]* We'll all remember him.

MRS. BRADY: Let the men do their work, girl.

As HARGREAVES *digs,* CHILTON *goes off, right, towards the body.*

CHILTON, *coming back:* Cold. – *Dead* cold. Gettin' colder by the minute.

SGT. WADE: Did you *have* to?

CHILTON: Don't want to bury no 'live man.

SGT. WADE: Well, help bury a dead one. Take a turn on the shovel.

CHILTON *takes the shovel and digs. After a moment, he pauses, wipes his face with both sleeves, and scrapes hair back out of his eyes.*

CHILTON, *smiling at* JUDY: Would've shaved, miss, if I'd had the time!

HARGREAVES: And a razor. And somebody standin' over you with a whip.

CHILTON, *to* HARGREAVES, *as he continues to dig:* When's the last time you cleaned *your*self?

HARGREAVES: Some don't get as dirty as others.

CHILTON, *pausing:* Some don't work as hard, either.

SGT. WADE, *to* CHILTON: Just dig the damn' grave.

All are silent, as CHILTON *digs.*

CHILTON, *pausing, and addressing* MRS. BRADY: I was wonderin', ma'am – could you spare another mug of that water?

MRS. BRADY: Certainly. *[To* JUDY.*]* Bring another pitcher, will you?

CHILTON, *to* JUDY: If you have to go to the well for it, I'd be glad to carry the bucket.

JUDY, *as she goes off, right, with the pitcher:* I've carried many a bucket. I don't need any help.

SGT. WADE: Keep to it, Chilton. *[Nodding at the grave.]* It ain't half dug.

HARGREAVES, *chuckling, to* CHILTON: You 'bout as subtle as a forty pounder!

CHILTON: Shut up, or you'll be eatin' this shovel.

SGT. WADE, *sharply:* Save your breath, you two. There's a lot of diggin' yet.

CHILTON *digs on, in silence.*

MRS. BRADY: I'm glad you brought him to us, Sergeant. He'll be here always, now.

SGT. WADE: What's left of 'im, yes'm.

MRS. BRADY: There's a great deal left of him. – Today's his birthday, you know.
SGT. WADE: No'm, I didn't.
MRS. BRADY, *nodding:* It's the Martinmass. He was named "Martin" for the saint.
HARGREAVES: Today's the *what?*
MRS. BRADY: The Martinmass. It's a feast of the church.
HARGREAVES: Oh.
CHILTON: I never knew his first name.
HARGREAVES: *Some* people have 'em.
CHILTON: I got one. John. That's mine.
HARGREAVES: Do tell!
SGT. WADE: I knew his first name was Martin. Saw it writ down somewhere once.
HARGREAVES: You can read, can you?
SGT. WADE: *Some* things. I can write, too.
HARGREAVES: Do tell!
MRS. BRADY: I don't have anything to mark it with – the grave. But I'll get something.
CHILTON, *as he digs:* Damn' few gets a marker these days.
MRS. BRADY, *nodding:* He'll have one.
SGT. WADE: That's good of you, ma'am.
MRS. BRADY: Not so good as it ought to be! I can't afford *that.*
JUDY *re-enters, right, with the pitcher.* HARGREAVES *picks up the mug from the ground and holds it out.* JUDY *pours it full.*
HARGREAVES, *grinning at* CHILTON *as he drinks:* To your health, sir!
CHILTON, *dropping the shovel:* You wouldn't have it, if I hadn't asked. Give it here!
HARGREAVES: When I'm finished.
SGT. WADE: Easy, you two!

JUDY *meanwhile has put down the pitcher and picked up the shovel. All stare in silence as she starts awkwardly to dig. After a moment* SGT. WADE *goes to her and grasps the shovel. Briefly his hand touches hers.*

SGT. WADE: That's our work, miss. You shouldn't be –

JUDY: I want to! – just to remember I had a part in it.

Once more they all watch as JUDY *digs. At length* SGT. WADE *takes the shovel from her.*

SGT. WADE: Too heavy! Too heavy for you, miss. Let me do it.

JUDY, *as she relinquishes the shovel:* You're right. I'm not very good at it.

SGT. WADE: But you wanted to! That's decent of you.

HARGREAVES: The lieutenant brung out decency in unexpected quarters. Why, even Chilton used to wash his face for Sunday service!

CHILTON: Some's lucky they still got a face to wash.

SGT. WADE, *holding out the shovel:* Hargreaves! Here! *Your* turn.

HARGREAVES *takes the shovel and digs.*

SGT. WADE, *to* JUDY: What was it he talked about last night?

JUDY: Oh, different things. God – us (Mrs. Brady and me) – some legend from the place where he was born.

SGT. WADE: You sat up with him – you and Mrs. Brady – all night long?

JUDY *nods.*

SGT. WADE: Must have been hard on you.

JUDY: Harder on *him.*

SGT. WADE: I'm glad he – he had his last night with good folk.

JUDY: If he did, it's because he helped us be that way.

MRS. BRADY, *wearily:* I'm afraid I must go inside. Come, girl. You need some rest yourself. I'd almost forgot we haven't seen bed since night before last.

HARGREAVES, *leaning on the shovel:* Ain't *none* of us slept in a right smart while – ma'am.
SGT. WADE, *quietly: Dig*, dammit, Hargreaves!
MRS. BRADY, *nodding:* You must be exhausted, all of you. Hungry, too. Come up to the house when you're done. I can't hold a 'wake' for your lieutenant, but I'll have something for you.
CHILTON, *wiping his mouth on his sleeve:* Yes, *ma'am*!
HARGREAVES: He means we're most grateful, ma'am.
MRS. BRADY: May you feel so *afterwards*! I haven't much to offer. Come along, girl.
The women go off, right, together. The three soldiers stare after them a moment. Then, at an impatient gesture from SGT. WADE, HARGREAVES *starts to dig again. The stage slowly darkens.*

Scene 3.

Scene: Kitchen of THE WIDOW BRADY'S *house.*
Time: A few minutes after Scene 2.

The curtain rises on an ample but austere kitchen. In the rear wall a door to the outside, left of center, leads off to a small back porch. Right of center a large window looks out onto the porch and, beyond it, the garden. Against the rear wall, between the back door and the window, stands a deal dresser with shelves for plates and cutlery. In the left wall a door leads off to the front hall and the rest of the house. Against the right wall stands a wood-burning stove with oven. At right, upstage of the stove, is a small wooden table. Pots, pans, and utensils clutter the small table and hang on the wall, right, to either side of the stove. A small pile of wood lies on the floor, left of the stove. Downstage center a long wooden table stands roughly parallel to the footlights. At its left end is a straight-backed chair. Near it, on the upstage side of the table, is a second chair. Other chairs of the same homemade design stand against the left and rear walls of the kitchen.

When the curtain rises, JUDY, *discovered right, puts a piece of wood in the stove and busies herself with pots and pans.* MRS. BRADY *enters through the door, left, carrying a bedsheet in her arms. She appears exhausted.*

MRS. BRADY, *as she throws the sheet over the table, downstage center:* What do we have to give them, Judy?
JUDY, *as she works, her back to* MRS. BRADY: There's half a ham in the smokehouse.
MRS. BRADY, *nodding wearily:* Bring it. And there must be some side meat left. It can go in the greens.
JUDY, *turning around and catching sight of the table cover:* Why – it's a sheet!
MRS. BRADY, *as she moves plates from the dresser to the table:* It is.
JUDY, *abstractedly:* From –?
MRS. BRADY, *setting out the plates:* From Hiram's bed. I remembered we gave our last tablecloth for bandages. We can't serve on a bare table, now can we?
JUDY: But Robert's sheets went – went with the chaplain. And now Hiram's –! When your sons come, you won't have bedding for 'em.
MRS. BRADY, *as she works:* Maybe they won't all be coming.
JUDY, *taking a step toward her:* Won't – won't be coming?
MRS. BRADY: Go get the ham girl. The men will be here shortly.
JUDY: You – you've given up hope?
MRS. BRADY: Never! But hope has a way of giving *you* up.
JUDY: What's that mean?
MRS. BRADY: It means that hope alone isn't enough to live on. And without life there can *be* no hope. Right now you and I – these men who've done us service – we must all go on living.

JUDY: But they *will* come back! Jared will! You made me believe it!

MRS. BRADY, *shaking her head and smiling:* You made your*self* believe it – just as I did. But believe away, child! I'll help you. If you believe hard enough, why, he *will* come back! – You just may not know him, when he does.

JUDY: Will *you* know him?

MRS. BRADY: If I'm still above ground, I'm sure I will! Look to the fire, now. They may want to warm themselves. And bring the ham.

JUDY: That ham's the last we've got.

MRS. BRADY, *nodding:* Bring it. – You and I, we'll live on *some*thing – even if we have to eat grass, like Nebuchadnezzar.

JUDY: Like "Nebooka" – *who?*

MRS. BRADY: He was an evil king in the Bible. Just think of him as a Yankee. – And bring a potato or two. That flour we've been saving – make some biscuits. And stretch it, child: roll 'em thin. – I wish we had some butter!

JUDY: Ham gravy 'll do.

MRS. BRADY: Yes. Yes, it'll have to.

JUDY: Shall I fetch the jug from the cellar?

MRS. BRADY: No. Too early in the day for whiskey. They shouldn't have it, even if they ask. – And I'll be needing some myself, when they're gone. Just fetch another bucket from the well. They can take fresh water with them. – Well, go on! I'll do the table.

JUDY *goes out the back door.* MRS. BRADY *finishes setting the table. She draws up chairs for five, two on the upstage side, one opposite them downstage, and one at either end. The effort tires her out. She sinks down in the chair at the end of the table, left. She rests her elbows on the table, her head in her hands. On the porch* JUDY *is heard, putting down a bucket of water. She re-enters through the back door with the piece of ham and two potatoes. She stops, lays them on the small table, right, and stares at* MRS. BRADY.

MRS. BRADY, *rousing herself suddenly:* No time to bake that meat. Just fry it up. You'll have to do it, girl. I'm worn to a whittling! And roll those biscuits thin.

JUDY *goes to her and puts a hand on her shoulder.*

JUDY: I'll do it, Mrs. Brady. Rest yourself.

MRS. BRADY *nods.* JUDY *goes to work at the stove and the small table.* MRS. BRADY *slumps back in her chair.*

MRS. BRADY, *wearily, almost to herself:* My sons! – My sons! – I hope some one fed *them* – before Malvern Hill! *[Falls asleep.]*

JUDY *prepares the food in silence. Occasionally she looks over her shoulder at* MRS. BRADY. *Once,* JUDY *pauses and goes to the window. When she goes a second time to the window, she stops, then moves to the back door and holds it open.* SGT. WADE *enters.*

JUDY, *quietly:* I saw you coming up the path. Are you done?

SGT. WADE: Almost. They'll be here when they've covered the grave.

JUDY, *with a finger to her lips and nodding at* MRS. BRADY: Speak softly. She's asleep. *[Closes the door.]* I thought you'd wake her if you knocked.

SGT. WADE, *looking at* MRS. BRADY: She sick?

JUDY, *going back to work:* Just tired. She doesn't sleep much at night any more.

SGT. WADE, *nodding:* And I guess *last* night took its toll.

JUDY, *as she works:* It did.

SGT. WADE: Must have been hard – you two alone here with *him.*

JUDY: It was more than that. When we saw you and your men coming this morning, we thought you were her sons.

SGT. WADE: Her sons?

JUDY: Her three sons we'd been told were killed. She won't believe it – thinks they'll all come back one day. I sit up watching with her sometimes. We thought you three were they.

SGT. WADE, *making a helpless gesture with his hat:* Well, that – that's an awful thing!

JUDY, *not looking at him:* It's an awful thing you *weren't.*

SGT. WADE: Her old man – she said he's gone, too?

JUDY: Long ago.

SGT. WADE: The three boys her only –?

JUDY: That's right.

SGT. WADE: You not her daughter?

JUDY: Daughter-in-*law*, I would have been. Her youngest son –! *[Stops abruptly.]*

SGT. WADE: I'm sorry.

JUDY: Yes, well – we all are. *[Takes a plate of ham off the stovetop.]* Here. You can put this on the table, if you will. Don't burn yourself.

SGT. WADE *takes the plate by the potholders* JUDY *offers.*

SGT. WADE, *putting the plate on the table:* I – I mean, I'm really sorry – sorry this all had to happen as it did.

JUDY, *pausing to glance out the window:* I guess it had to happen *some* way.

SGT. WADE: How you mean?

JUDY, *shrugging:* Too long a story. I see the others coming.

SGT. WADE: Miss – er – Miss –?

JUDY, *turning to him:* Judy. My name's Judy.

SGT. WADE: Well, Judy, I wanted to tell you, I was touched – touched that you felt like having a part in the burial. Lieutenant Fergus meant a lot to the men and me.

JUDY: He must have. *[Glances at* MRS. BRADY.*]* He meant a lot to us, too.

SGT. WADE, *awkwardly:* I – I'd like to feel I could come back here some day, after the fightin's done – to pay my respects to him – to his memory, you know.

JUDY: I'm sure Mrs. Brady would welcome you.

SGT. WADE *nods thoughtfully. The sound of boots on the back porch jars him.*

SGT. WADE: Will you be here yourself?

JUDY: I'll be with Mrs. Brady as long as she needs me.

SGT. WADE: I mean I –

JUDY *looks at him quickly. A heavy knock sounds at the back door.* MRS. BRADY *jerks upright.*

MRS. BRADY, *looking about her:* Good heaven! Is it finished?

SGT. WADE: Yes, ma'am. He's in the ground and covered.

JUDY *goes to the door. She lets in* CHILTON *and* HARGREAVES.

MRS. BRADY, *rising wearily:* Ought to be buried myself – sitting here asleep while all of you work! *[To the men.]* Come in. Warm yourselves.

CHILTON *and* HARGREAVES *make no move toward the stove. They eye the plate of ham, then each other, and edge closer to the table.*

MRS. BRADY *goes to the stove.*

MRS. BRADY, *to* JUDY: Is the food –

JUDY, *quickly:* Yes'm. It's finished, too.

MRS. BRADY: Biscuits done?

JUDY, *nodding:* Done to a turn – and thin as smoke.

MRS. BRADY, *lifting the lid on a pot:* Collards seem to be steaming. *[Raises her voice as she stirs the greens.]* Well, seat yourselves when you're ready.

CHILTON *and* HARGREAVES *scramble into the two upstage chairs at the table.* MRS. BRADY *turns at the noise.* SGT. WADE *clenches his fist at the men.*

SGT. WADE, *in a low voice:* Don't touch a damned thing, either of you. *[Turns to* MRS. BRADY *and* JUDY.*]* We'll wait till you can join us, ma'am.

MRS. BRADY, *going back to the far left seat at the table:* It's not a meal to be fancy about. I won't keep you. *[Sits down.]* I'm

Mrs. Brady. *[*JUDY *puts biscuits and a pot of greens on the table and sits in the downstage chair to* MRS. BRADY'S left.*]* And this is Miss Judy Barden.

The men nod and murmur "How' do."

MRS. BRADY *to* SGT. WADE: Did you say something over him – out there, when you'd finished?

SGT. WADE, *sitting in the chair at right end of table:* Er – no, ma'am. None of us knew anything to say.

MRS. BRADY: *I'm* not much on praying, either. But you knew him better than Miss Judy and I. If you felt like saying something now –

CHILTON, *licking his lips as he eyes the ham:* What's that ol' hymn they always sing?

HARGREAVES: "Rock of Ages."

CHILTON, *turning to him:* That's it! How's it go?

HARGREAVES: I cain't sing.

CHILTON: Yo' dern fool! Jes' *say* it.

HARGREAVES, *slowly:* Cain't remember it, much. "Rock of Ages – cleft for me." – That's all I know.

SGT. WADE: They's somethin' in it about "Should my tears forever flow, should my zeal no longer know –"

MRS. BRADY: "Languor," Sergeant!

SGT. WADE: Ma'am?

MRS. BRADY: I believe the word is "languor": "should my zeal no languor know."

SGT. WADE: Maybe they sing it different in your church. Anyway, that's as far as I can get.

MRS. BRADY: It's far enough. Please start.

CHILTON *and* HARGREAVES *serve themselves quickly and attack their plates.* SGT. WADE *offers to serve* MRS. BRADY.

MRS. BRADY: After you, Sergeant. It's a long time since I've had young men at my table.

HARGREAVES: Long time since *we've* had a meal like this – hot ham gravy! And sittin' down to a table that ain't nekkid!

CHILTON: A year anyway.

MRS. BRADY: I hope it won't be that long again.

CHILTON, *shrugging as he eats:* God knows!

HARGREAVES: He means he hopes so, too, ma'am, but –

CHILTON: But God *knows*! – And who asked *you* to be always sayin' what I mean?

HARGREAVES: You ain't very good at it yourself.

CHILTON: So? When I want your opinion, I'll tell it to you.

SGT. WADE: Eat up, you two. We got to be gettin' back.

The men eat in silence for a moment.

HARGREAVES: You know, it ain't "Rock of Ages," but there was one thing I *did* think of, out there while we dug.

SGT. WADE: What's that?

HARGREAVES: I was wishin' some o' them infantry types had been here. Wasn't it General Harvey Hill said, "Who ever seen a dead cavalryman?"

CHILTON: No. It was Powell Hill.

SGT. WADE: I believe it was Harvey. I heard it after the fightin' on the Peninsula.

CHILTON: I ain't seen many dead *generals* either. He's got a big mouth, whichever it was.

HARGREAVES: That ought to make him a hero o' your'n!

CHILTON: Not hardly. Too many Hills in this man's army.

SGT. WADE: No, not enough. They're good men, both.

CHILTON: Well, lots of others have said it, too. *[In a mocking tone.]* "Who ever seen a dead man wearin' spurs?" *[Stabs another biscuit off its platter with his knife.]* Hell, them infantry types got no manners.

SGT. WADE, *thoughtfully:* You know – you two give me an idea! What if we tell the regiment Lieutenant Fergus is still alive? They sure didn't *want* him to die.

CHILTON, *grinning at* SERGEANT WADE: That tickles me down to the toe! It would take some steam out o' ol' Doc Folton. He thinks he knows everything.

HARGREAVES, *grinning, too:* Yeah! Folton said he wasn't worth sewin' up. Let's tell 'em the lieutenant made it!

SGT. WADE: Of course, you'll have to clean that shovel till it looks like you could eat off it.

HARGREAVES: We may *have* to eat off it. Not many plates where *we're* goin'!

CHILTON: If I can't clean a shovel, I'll kiss my own elbow. They's lots o' stobs and standin' water this side o' camp.

SGT. WADE: But maybe some officer might come by to see him.

MRS. BRADY: I can take care of that. I'll say he's asleep – or just too weak to talk.

SGT. WADE, *nodding:* That's *good*! We won't be camped here long. We can say he's lingerin' – gettin' his rest. It'll mean somethin' to the regiment, just to think he ain't dead.

MRS. BRADY: It'll mean something to all of us.

SGT. WADE: Of course – they'll find out one of these days.

MRS. BRADY: But not for a while.

SGT. WADE: Well, let's go men. They'll be wonderin' where we are. Mind what you say when we get there: this'll have to rest with the three of *us*. Fill canteens before you go. Hop to it! I'll meet you out front.

CHILTON *crams one last biscuit into his mouth. Then he and* HARGREAVES *rise, murmuring thanks to* MRS. BRADY.

JUDY: There's a full bucket on the porch – funnel hanging under the eaves. I'll show you. *[Goes out the back door with the men.]*

SGT. WADE, *to* MRS. BRADY: I thank you, ma'am, for the three of us. I'm sorry the men made so much fuss. They're always scrappin'. They don't mean anything by it. They need to find some Yankees, so they can work it off.

MRS. BRADY: It's all right, Sergeant. My two oldest – Robert and Hiram – they were always arguing. Jared, the youngest – wasn't the arguing sort.

SGT. WADE, *nodding:* Well, I'm not much on arguments myself. After this big one with the North, I'll settle for a life of peace with all Virginia-kind.

MRS. BRADY: And how do you think it'll end, this big one with the North?

SGT. WADE, *grinning:* Ain't but one way, ma'am! We'll clean 'em off our land.

MRS. BRADY: I hope so – and soon!

SGT. WADE: Before the lieutenant's grave is green.

MRS. BRADY: Amen!

SGT. WADE *moves toward the back door.* JUDY *opens it from outside and comes in.*

SGT. WADE, *looking at her intently:* Goodbye, Judy. I'll remember –!

JUDY, *embarrassed:* Yes, I – I'll remember, too.

SGT. WADE: I mean – more than anything else – I'll remember the touch of your hand on that shovel. *[Goes out quickly.]*

JUDY *closes the door and walks slowly to the table.*

MRS. BRADY: Well! Not "Miss Judy," but just plain "Judy"!

JUDY: He said he'd be back – to pay his respects some day at the grave. I told him you'd be glad to let him.

MRS. BRADY, *smiling:* Of course, I will!

JUDY: Do you think – do you think he'll ever *be* back?

MRS. BRADY: I do. He seemed devoted to – to the lieutenant.

JUDY: I mean – do you think the three of 'em will live through?

MRS. BRADY, *rising and going to her:* Some one will. *Some* one has to survive this war! And – *[She smiles.]* – and "who ever seen a dead cavalryman?"

JUDY: You and I – we saw one.

MRS. BRADY: But *he* wasn't a cavalryman. He was a preacher. And besides –

JUDY: Besides –?

MRS. BRADY: Well, if the men of the 10th Virginia think he's still alive – why, *that's* something!
JUDY, *abstractedly:* You mean – besides, he's not *dead,* either!
MRS. BRADY, *smiling and putting her arm around* JUDY: Come, girl. Let's gather up what's left.
JUDY: It's hardly enough to save.
MRS. BRADY, *quietly:* It's enough. It *will* be – enough.
The two women begin to clear the table.

Curtain

ACT III.

Scene: Parlor and front porch of THE WIDOW BRADY'S *house, as in* ACT I.
Time: An afternoon in late April, 1865.

When the curtain rises, MRS. BRADY *is lying on the sofa. Her head rests against the arm to stage right. Her eyes are closed. A throw-rug hangs on the back of the sofa.* JUDY *enters by the front door of the house, closes the door behind her, then comes on through the double doorway into the parlor. She sees* MRS. BRADY, *stops, and raises one hand to her mouth.*

MRS. BRADY, *opening her eyes:* Well, what is it, child?

JUDY: Nothing! I mean – well, I never saw you lie out here like that!

MRS. BRADY: No. – No, it's *his* place, isn't it? Ever since that night, it's been *his* sofa. Well, it's mine again, I've come to think. I'm tired, girl. I'll rest myself.

JUDY: You're not – you're not sick?

MRS. BRADY, *waving her hand:* Just weary. Today more than most. Tuck that throw around my legs, will you?

JUDY: It's a warm afternoon. You sure you want –?

MRS. BRADY: Just do it! Don't argue with me.

JUDY, *as she tucks the throw around her:* Do you have a chill?

MRS. BRADY: I don't have anything – just the yeasty years that have gone and left me!

JUDY: You've never lain out like this in the daytime!

MRS. BRADY: Well, maybe I *should* have. Get used to it, girl. – What's the matter, staring at me like that? Don't you have something to do?

JUDY: I – I came to tell you there's a man here – says he wants to see you.

MRS. BRADY: A man? Who is it?

JUDY, *shaking her head:* I don't know. Never saw him before.
MRS. BRADY: He look like a friend?
JUDY: He's wearing gray breeches – what's left of 'em.
MRS. BRADY: That doesn't mean much, these days. You think he's a deserter?
JUDY, *shaking her head:* He doesn't seem to be running.
MRS. BRADY: If he didn't want *you*, there's nothing here for a man to steal, God knows! I don't feel much like talking, but – well, show him in.
JUDY *goes out to the front porch.* MRS. BRADY *closes her eyes and rests her head again on the arm of the sofa. She draws the throw up toward her chest and moves one hand to her throat.*
JUDY, *on the porch:* She says she'll see you. Come inside.
JUDY *re-enters and stands, left, facing the sofa and the door to the hall. A man in a black, tattered frock coat enters, left, via the porch and the hall door. His gray trousers are tucked into well-worn boots. He is tall, gaunt, and bearded. He holds a gray hat with yellow braid in his left hand. His canteen hangs from a shoulder strap. A military belt holds his coat together, but he has no weapon. When he sees* MRS. BRADY, *he stops and stands, center, at the foot of the sofa.*
MRS. BRADY, *rousing herself slightly:* Well? Have you business with me?
THE VISITOR: I believe I do.
MRS. BRADY: And what might it be?
THE VISITOR, *after a pause:* You're not in good health, Mrs. Brady. I can tell *that*, just from looking into your face.
MRS. BRADY: My face never *was* for looking at. Precious little a body can do about *that*! Precious less a physician can do now for the rest of me. But you didn't come here to tell me I look ill.
THE VISITOR: No, though I – I thought it my duty.
MRS. BRADY: What else is your duty, if that's what brings you?
THE VISITOR: It's not exactly a duty – more a labor of love.

MRS. BRADY: Who are you?

THE VISITOR: I'm Doctor Henry Folton, lately regimental surgeon to the 10th Virginia Cavalry.

MRS. BRADY: "Lately"?

DR. FOLTON: We've been disbanded.

MRS. BRADY: Disbanded?

DR. FOLTON: Haven't you heard? The war's over.

JUDY *takes a step back in surprise.*

MRS. BRADY, *sitting up suddenly:* It's over?

DR. FOLTON, *nodding wearily:* Some days ago. I've forgotten how many.

MRS. BRADY: You surrendered?

DR. FOLTON, *shaking his head slightly:* Didn't have to. We were off on the scout – got word from Appomattox that General Lee and the army had surrendered. We were told to disband – go home.

MRS. BRADY *lies down again, drawing the throw up over her.*

JUDY, *to* DR. FOLTON: It's really over – the war?

DR. FOLTON: I think some Southern troops in the West are still under arms. They're too few and too far to get to, now. And there wasn't much left of the old Tenth to try.

JUDY: You had a Sergeant Wade? – Sergeant Calvin Wade?

DR. FOLTON, *looking at her:* Yes.

JUDY: He's alive?

DR. FOLTON, *nodding:* Last I saw of him! *[Turning to* MRS. BRADY.*]* He told me you have a remarkable spring, Mrs. Brady – clearest, freshest water he ever tasted. I could use some, if you'd be good enough.

MRS. BRADY: We've got the finest well in four counties – sweet – cold as if it came from the Arctic. Judy! Fetch us a pitcher of fresh.

DR. FOLTON, *to* JUDY: I'd be obliged to you, miss.

JUDY: Certainly. *[Goes out, right, through the hall.]*

DR. FOLTON: Mrs. Brady, while the girl is gone – there's something I'd like to say.

MRS. BRADY: You haven't said enough? It's nothing worse –?

DR. FOLTON: That depends.

MRS. BRADY: On me?

DR. FOLTON, *nodding:* Perhaps – and on the girl.

MRS. BRADY: Well, say it, man. I hear you.

DR. FOLTON: You may not know it, but in his last letter to her, Sergeant Wade asked Judy – Miss Barden – to be his wife.

MRS. BRADY: *Did* he now?

DR. FOLTON: And he received no letter back. Do you know whether she wrote him?

MRS. BRADY: She answers when she's spoken to. I imagine she made reply to a letter of that sort, if she knew where to send it.

DR. FOLTON, *nodding:* But do you know whether she did or not?

MRS. BRADY: I've no idea.

DR. FOLTON: Mrs. Brady! It's important.

MRS. BRADY: The girl doesn't tell me all she does – or thinks. We're close, but we're not mother and daughter.

DR. FOLTON: It's important because – you see, he was wounded.

MRS. BRADY: Wounded? Badly?

DR. FOLTON: Yes. His arm –

MRS. BRADY: Not – not his right arm?

DR. FOLTON: Yes. His right arm.

MRS. BRADY, *sitting up:* He didn't lose it?

DR. FOLTON, *nodding:* It had to come off. I amputated it myself.

MRS. BRADY: You don't mean –!

DR. FOLTON: I do. A minie ball struck him above the elbow – compound fracture. I couldn't save the arm. And his only thought, when he came out of it, was that Judy wouldn't want him now – even if she *had* wanted him before. He felt he had no right to hold her to a promise she may have made when he was whole and healthy.

MRS. BRADY, *absently, as she lies down again:* No right –?

DR. FOLTON: He was a farmer before the war – wanted to go back to the land when it was over. After the amputation he feared he might be useless trying to farm with just one hand. He's a strong man, though – and resourceful. He can make it if he has the will – if he has the help of a good woman.

MRS. BRADY: He's a strong man, I know.

DR. FOLTON: He's made a fair recovery – gotten so he can dress himself, without much help. But the loss of a limb affects people –

MRS. BRADY: What do you mean?

DR. FOLTON, *shrugging:* Some it takes the wind out of – makes them think they can't go on. Makes them feel the world has changed, just because *they* have – that life will be the harder on them – that people won't accept them now, either for what they were or for what, in their perhaps limited way, they may become.

MRS. BRADY: The world – *our* world – *has* changed. Hearts are harder for it.

DR. FOLTON: Not his.

MRS. BRADY: How do you know? If losing an arm has taken the wind out of him –

DR. FOLTON: Because he *cares* about this girl, whether or not she cares for him – or used to.

MRS. BRADY: What about his people? Has he any prospects?

DR. FOLTON: He has no parents. An older brother who farms, south of here, will take him in. But he's always wanted to be his own man. He had great responsibility in the 10th Virginia. He was regimental sergeant-major when he took that bullet. After the war – if he survived – he wanted to go on being the man he had been. He wanted a place of his own. Without an arm he hasn't much hope of that.

MRS. BRADY: I knew a farmer once, lost his hand in a logging accident. He kept on working till that other arm grew thick as a ham. Over the years he got along as if he'd never been hurt. Used to say he didn't see why God *gave* a man two hands in the first place.

DR. FOLTON: No doubt, he had the support of a wife – perhaps children, too.

MRS. BRADY: He did.

DR. FOLTON: Well, Sergeant Wade has neither.

MRS. BRADY: As yet.

DR. FOLTON, *nodding:* As yet.

MRS. BRADY: You think he won't?

DR. FOLTON: Do *you*?

MRS. BRADY, *closing her eyes:* It's not my business to think. He must take it up with *her*.

DR. FOLTON, *shaking his head:* He's a proud man, Mrs. Brady. And a deeply decent one. He doesn't want to force the girl – doesn't want to play on her pity. He won't insist that she tie herself to him. I believe he loves her very much – too much to compel her to choose a life that may leave both of them wanting. After all, there *are* able-bodied men.

MRS. BRADY: *Are* there? – I've lost more than an arm in this war, Doctor.

DR. FOLTON: I understand. Sergeant Wade told me about your sons.

MRS. BRADY: I've lost some years, too – strength – patience – hope for the future.

DR. FOLTON: We all have, Mrs. Brady.

MRS. BRADY: You sound as if you're still doing your duty! Why're you telling me this?

DR. FOLTON: Because Sergeant Wade wanted me to. He's out there waiting, near your gate. He wants to know whether

Judy will have him – as he is, without repining. If she will, he'll come to her. If not, he wants to journey on with me to the south. I understand how he feels. I don't want to see him hurt any more. If she doesn't want to marry him – or if she did, but doesn't want to now – he would like to go on without seeing her.

MRS. BRADY: You've taken charge of him, have you?

DR. FOLTON: I suppose I have. After I cut off his arm, I left him with some women in the schoolhouse that had been our hospital. I went back there and took him up, when the end came. I have family in Richmond, but I told Wade I would go on with him to his brother's. I won't leave him till I see him with his own.

MRS. BRADY: Just you and he! What about those other two – Chilton – Hargreaves?

DR. FOLTON: Both dead. A brush with Sheridan's cavalry, west of here.

MRS. BRADY: God, have they left us *no* one!

DR. FOLTON: They've left us *one* good man I know of.

MRS. BRADY, *wearily:* You'll have to take it up with *her*, Doctor Folton – you or he will.

DR. FOLTON: He won't see her, ma'am. He wants her to have a chance to make up her mind before she sees him.

MRS. BRADY: That's asking a lot. He may have changed. I mean – in other ways.

DR. FOLTON: Oh, he's changed, all right. But it's all inside. You'd never know there was anything different about him – except for the empty sleeve. He's lost some faith in himself, it's true. But his soul is all there. Only – it'll take another soul to bring him back – all the way back. – I've come to agree with him. If it's not to be Judy Barden, I think we should travel on without his seeing her.

MRS. BRADY: Then *you* ask her.

DR. FOLTON: But you *know* the girl!

MRS. BRADY, *waving her hand feebly:* No matter! If she doesn't want him, she won't listen to me.
DR. FOLTON: But she may! Will you do it for him?
MRS. BRADY, *slowly:* I would do what I could for any one who'd fought for us. – But I'm too far gone now to have much sway with the young.
DR. FOLTON: Will you just tell her? – talk to her about him?
MRS. BRADY, *exhausted:* I'll talk to her. – She must decide for herself.
DR. FOLTON: It's all I ask! – He's out there waiting with my horse. We take turns, riding. He's good on his feet, like an infantryman – a long sight better than I am! And he's learned to handle the horse with his one good hand. I'll go back to him in a moment. We agreed on a sign. If he sees your front door open and the girl standing in it, he'll come to the house. If not, in half an hour we'll both be gone.
MRS. BRADY: Ah, you give me half an hour!
DR. FOLTON: If the girl's answer is "no," I think he and I should be well away from here by dark.
MRS. BRADY, *weakly:* Half an hour!
DR. FOLTON, *as they both hear* JUDY *coming in from the kitchen:* Of course, if you think it worthwhile, we could return in the morning.
MRS. BRADY, *as* JUDY *comes in from the hall with a pitcher of water and a cup:* No. – No: tomorrow is too late.
DR. FOLTON: Do you mean – ?
MRS. BRADY: I mean, if you give me half an hour, I'll take it!
JUDY, *staring at* MRS. BRADY: Are you all right?
MRS. BRADY, *laughing quietly:* Is *any*one? – Give the doctor a drink, girl! We must think of our visitor!
JUDY *pours the cup full and offers it.*
DR. FOLTON, *taking the cup:* Ah, from the well of life! *[Drinks.]* By heaven, that's good! I thank you both. Water like

this would make a man think we'd won! *[Finishes off the cupful.]* May I take some in my canteen?

JUDY, *offering the pitcher:* Please. Take it all.

DR. FOLTON, *as he fills his canteen:* Thank you. It'll stand me well, on the way to Richmond.

JUDY: Are you off, then?

DR. FOLTON: I will be, shortly. – I believe our chaplain, Martin Fergus, is buried here?

JUDY: You *knew* – ? You knew he'd died?

DR. FOLTON, *with a sad smile:* I think I was the only one – for quite some time. They made a good story of it, those three. The rest of the men believed he was here, recovering. I'm afraid I knew he couldn't survive. I said so to Sergeant Wade the night he brought him here. The regiment *wanted* to think Chaplain Fergus was still with us. Simple men, most of them. Good-hearted, too. I let them think it. They had little enough to believe in, toward the end.

MRS. BRADY: I meant to get him a stone. I've not been able to. Nothing but a cross of sticks over him now – that and a growth of grass.

DR. FOLTON: I'd like to see it, if I may. I'm in need of inspiration myself. Our chaplain – well, he meant something to me.

MRS. BRADY: He meant something to all of us.

JUDY: It's just out behind the house. I'll take you.

DR. FOLTON, *stopping her:* That's all right. I know where it is. Sergeant Wade told me – after we disbanded. Out there at the end of the orchard – by the little copse of locust trees. You were good to offer, miss. I'll find it. I'd like to go alone. *[To* MRS. BRADY.*]* My respects, ma'am. God be with you. *[Goes out through the hall and off the porch, having closed the front door behind him.]*

MRS. BRADY, *quietly, as* Dr. FOLTON *leaves:* If he's *any*where!

JUDY: Was that why he came? – his "labor of love," to see the chaplain's grave?

MRS. BRADY: Maybe he came to see mine.

JUDY, *aghast:* Mrs. Brady!

MRS. BRADY: Oh, don't take on, child. I can't abide doctors. You never hear good news from one of *them.*

JUDY: He *seemed* an honest soul. Maybe he'll stop by the house before he goes. We could spare him a slice or two of bread.

MRS. BRADY: He didn't come for bread.

JUDY: What *did* he come for?

MRS. BRADY: Sit down, girl. Come: sit down here beside me.

JUDY *draws up a chair and sits, facing,* MRS. BRADY.

JUDY: What is it? Are you feeling cold again?

MRS. BRADY: I'm warm enough for what I have to do. – Tell me, girl: with the war over and no news at all, you're not still thinking about my son, Jared, are you?

JUDY: Aren't you?

MRS. BRADY: I think about all of them – all my sons – every day. But I've given up thinking they'll be back.

JUDY: No!

MRS. BRADY: I have. I've told you to do the same. They won't be back.

JUDY: I don't believe it!

MRS. BRADY: You'd better. It's three years now. We would have seen them, if they were still alive. We would have heard *some*thing! You've not seen me watching for them any more.

JUDY: But – but you've been too tired!

MRS. BRADY: We're both too tired. I'm wasted away with watching. I don't want *you* to be.

JUDY: I'm not too tired. I believe he'll come.

MRS. BRADY: Tell me, Judy: how did you leave it with that Sergeant Wade?

JUDY: "Leave it"? We're friends. He wrote me the nicest letters. We're good friends, I hope.

MRS. BRADY: No more than that?

JUDY: Well, I – I think *he* wanted it to be something more.

MRS. BRADY: He asked you to marry him, didn't he?

JUDY: I never told you that!

MRS. BRADY: Why didn't you tell me?

JUDY: Because you know I'm promised! I'm promised to Jared Brady, your son!

MRS. BRADY: You can't be promised to a dead man.

JUDY: He's *not* dead!

MRS. BRADY: How can I make you believe it, child? He's gone from us forever – like my husband – like my two eldest. *I'll* mourn them, all of them, for the both of us. – I have a right to be a widow. You have none. You must earn the right, if widowhood's your lot. Take it and welcome, if it comes. But you must live till then – live and work and do your woman's part. Here, in this backwater of Virginia, you and I, we've eked out an existence in a dying land. But *you* must do more than exist. You must raise up sons to the Virginia that will be.

JUDY: What are you telling me?

MRS. BRADY: I'm telling you he's come back, your Sergeant Wade. And through no fault of yours, he still wants to marry you.

JUDY, *rising from her chair:* How do you –? It's what that doctor said, isn't it? – that Doctor Folton. It's why he came here!

MRS. BRADY: That's part of it.

JUDY: There's something more?

MRS. BRADY: There is. But suppose you tell me whether you'll have Sergeant Wade.

JUDY, *turning and taking a step down left:* Well – I'm sure he's a good person.

MRS. BRADY: So am I.

JUDY, *facing her:* And you want me to marry him?

MRS. BRADY: I want you to marry *some* one. He's here and he's willing. And you're not for all markets.

JUDY: You're telling me I'm not bound to wait for Jared?

MRS. BRADY: He's taken from us, child. You've been *un*bound a long time already.

JUDY: You said there was something more –?

MRS. BRADY, *with a low sigh:* Yes, there's something more. – I won't be with you much longer.

JUDY, *sitting quickly and taking her hand: Mrs. Brady*!

MRS. BRADY, *taking her hand back:* Hush, now! I'm not going this minute! I've got too much to do.

JUDY, *almost in tears:* Mrs. Brady, no! Don't say such a thing!

MRS. BRADY: Get hold of yourself, girl. You'll send me off if you carry on! I won't stay for crying over me. I'm not worth it. – And you'll need your tears for other things.

JUDY, *trying to collect herself:* Oh, Mrs. Brady!

MRS. BRADY: Stop it! Stop it, I tell you. A grown woman, and carrying on like a school girl! – You're a fine, strapping piece of Eve's flesh, you are. You've done most of the work here, ever since you came. You've got more strength than sense – and more emotion than either. It'll come in handy, when you aim it right. And your target's ready and waiting.

JUDY: Oh, Mrs. Brady! Don't make fun of me!

MRS. BRADY, *more tenderly:* I'm not, girl. I'm trying to make a woman of you. If I'm to leave, I'll leave much easier, knowing you're with a decent man.

JUDY, *hesitant:* After all this time, loving Jared –!

MRS. BRADY: In his time and place, Jared was good for you – and you for him. But that's no more. Time – along with our poor power to tell it – has a way of running out.

JUDY: And – and it would make you happy to see me marry Sergeant Wade?

MRS. BRADY: Happier than to see you left here alone.

JUDY, *slowly:* Left – *here* – ?

MRS. BRADY: Yes, *here*! I have no heirs any more. If you marry a man I approve, this place, such as it is, I leave to you.
JUDY, *overwhelmed:* Oh, Mrs. Brady! – Mrs. Brady, I never expected –! I mean, you've always been so generous to me. – Oh, you didn't have to say that, Mrs. Brady! *[Starts to cry.]*
MRS. BRADY: Well, now, maybe I didn't. But it's how I feel, and there's no *harm* in saying it. This place is small, but it has two things that make it rich – the well and the dead lieutenant. He taught me something, that one! Taught me how to die, if nothing else. You must buy him a stone, Judy. Promise me you will, if you ever have the money.
JUDY, *controlling herself with an effort:* A stone – of course! Yes! Of course, I will! *We* will, you and I!
MRS. BRADY: There's something else you must do.
JUDY: Yes, Mrs. Brady. What is it?
MRS. BRADY: You must learn to live and be satisfied with what comes. Don't ask – don't hope for everything. My own three sons I sent to the war. If only one comes back to me now – and he, marked for life – I must be content. War does leave its mark – on every*thing* and every*body*. It takes its toll and gives no change. War – death – they're merciless as life itself. And *you* must be as merciless as they are. Sickness, injury, separation – they're all a part of life: they have no pity about them. And you must have no pity *for* them – or for yourself when they touch you. Hold to whatever good thing you have. Let the bad be its own and only friend.
JUDY: Are you – are you telling me there's still something more?
MRS. BRADY, *impatiently:* Yes, there's something more! There's always something more! – I feel very warm all of a sudden. From chills to fever on an April day! Yes! Go, open the front-hall door for me. A breeze may be stirring.
JUDY *goes out to the hall and opens the front door.*

MRS. BRADY: That's right. Yes. Stand there. Maybe fresh air will come. I have trouble catching my breath in here. Too much talking! I leave the talking to you young. I've *had* my time for talking. *[*JUDY *moves as if to go to her.]* No, don't come back. Stand there! Give your strength to the living, not the dead. Let all the green things grow and blow and cover the earth again! – Let it come, whatever it is!

JUDY *stands at the door, watching* MRS. BRADY. *She takes a tentative step back toward the sofa as* MRS. BRADY *subsides.* SGT. WADE *suddenly appears, left, and walks up on to the porch. He is hatless; his hair shows gray at the temples. Otherwise he looks as he did before, except for the empty sleeve pinned to the front of his coat.* JUDY *hears his footsteps and turns.*

JUDY: Oh! – Oh, my God! – What have they done to you? *[Steps toward him, hesitates a moment, then throws her arms around his neck.]* My God, what have they done –? She never –! Oh! Oh! *[Sobs into his shoulder.]*

SGT. WADE, *embracing her with his left arm:* It's all right, Judy! It's all right now! – I've gained two arms for the one I lost!

JUDY *continues to cry. They stand holding each other, oblivious, as* MRS. BRADY's *head falls to one side. Her hand drops lifeless to the floor.*

Curtain

A MODERN ROMANCE

A Play in One Act

THE CHARACTERS

HARVEY HARCOURT, a member of the United States Senate

MRS. HARCOURT, his wife

ELLEN HARCOURT, his daughter

CHARLEY MORTON, a guest

A MODERN ROMANCE

Scene: The library of SENATOR HARCOURT'S *home in Washington, D. C.*
Time: Jimmy Carter's presidency—an evening in early spring, when SENATOR HARCOURT *is giving a party in honor of his daughter. The stage darkens once to denote the passage of several hours.*

The curtain rises on the library of the home of SENATOR HARVEY HARCOURT, *who is living in Washington while the Senate is in session. A fireplace (with a mantlepiece above it) and a high bookcase are on the right. French windows open onto a terrace at the back. A table surmounted by a mirror stands at the back of the room to the left of the French windows. Another bookcase stands to the left of the table, and a doorway leads off downstage left to the rest of the house. A leather-upholstered sofa stands in the center of the stage with a small end-table to the left of it. Several chairs with lamps beside them are placed around the room. A small table with a telephone on it stands downstage right by the fireplace.*
The stage is empty as the curtain rises. The French windows and the door at left are open. Sounds of a party in progress come from time to time through the latter. It is late evening and dark outside.
ELLEN HARCOURT *runs in through the French windows from the terrace. She is a beautiful girl of twenty and wears a white evening gown. She sobs softly as she enters and throws herself on the sofa. She remains there, crying for a moment. Then she stops, sits up, and begins to dry her tears. Suddenly* MRS. HARCOURT, *an elderly woman with graying hair, enters through the door at left. She is also in evening dress.*
MRS. HARCOURT, *going to her daughter and sitting beside*

her on the sofa: Why, Ellen! What's the matter? I saw Brad come back into the drawingroom alone – I *thought* something must be wrong. What happened, dear?

ELLEN, *dabbing at her eyes with a handkerchief:* Nothing! Brad just asked me to marry him, that's all!

MRS. HARCOURT: Well, what's the matter with that? Why, half the girls in Washington are crazy about Brad Hemmings. They must be dying to have him ask *them* to marry him. I should think you'd be pleased!

ELLEN, *sarcastically:* Oh, yes, Mother! Brad is just the kind of person half of Washington *would* want to marry. And he *will* marry half the girls in Washington before he's through! – He's pleasant enough to be with – for a while – and to go riding, or swimming, or playing tennis with. But *marry* him –! Why, I'd feel safer married to Bluebeard!

MRS. HARCOURT: Well, I always thought Brad was very nice. And his mother and father are such dear friends of ours.

ELLEN: Oh, I suppose he's *nice*! – I only hope I didn't hurt his feelings. But I was too wrought up to have something like *that* happen to me. – He's not a bad person, really. It's just that he's so stuck on himself. And I wouldn't mind *that*, if there were some excuse for it. But honestly, I don't think he has sense enough to know Jimmy Carter from a hole in the ground!

MRS. HARCOURT: Well, my dear, that's not *his* fault. Few people in Washington do.

ELLEN: Just the same, he bores me. They *all* bore me. All those coffee-sipping, smooth-talking people in there.

MRS. HARCOURT: But, Ellen, you don't even know them all!

ELLEN: Well, I know all I care to. They're just like Brad Hemmings. Really, Mother – I almost died when Father told me I had to be here for this thing tonight. He knew I couldn't get out of it if he gave it in my honor. Oh, I appreciate it and all that – but you know how I hate parties. I stayed through dinner, but I just don't think I can bear any more! *[Very tenderly.]* And

Brad! Poor, poor Brad! I did *so* want to get away from that crowd of people. And when he asked me to go for a walk in the garden – well, I was closer to loving him than at any other time in my life! Oh, *why* did he have to go and spoil it all by asking me to marry him? *[Begins to sob again into her handkerchief.]*

MRS. HARCOURT, *putting an arm around* ELLEN *and patting her shoulder:* There, there, child! Don't cry any more. You don't have to come back to the party, if you don't want to. Go on upstairs and go to bed, if you like. I'm sure your father won't mind. As a matter of fact, I– er, I don't think he'll know anything about it.

ELLEN, *looking up from her handkerchief quickly:* Mother! You – you don't mean – Father's having "one of his nights" again!

MRS. HARCOURT: I'm afraid so, dear. But I've told Jarvis not to give him another drop – and if I stay close to him, I think I'll be able to keep him from going too far!

ELLEN: Oh, Mother, how awful! At his own party, too! Mother, has he – has he gotten to the point where he tells the story about the bearded lady and the sea captain?

MRS. HARCOURT: My dear, he told that one before dinner! He was about to launch into that awful thing about Aunt Harriet when I had to leave him and find you!

ELLEN, *getting up from the sofa and going over to the mirror:* How terrible! And he has to make a speech in the Senate tomorrow, too! I'll get ready and come with you as quickly as I can. My face is simply a mess!

MRS. HARCOURT, *getting up and going toward door, left:* No, Ellen, don't you worry. I'm the only one who can do anything with him when he gets this way. You run along to bed. *I* can take care of your father, all right! *[Goes out through door, left.]*

ELLEN, *standing in front of the mirror, begins to repair her make-up. A moment after* MRS. HARCOURT *leaves,*

CHARLEY MORTON *appears in the doorway. He is probably twenty-five years old and looks quite handsome in his black tuxedo. He enters slowly with an unlit cigarette in his mouth and a lighter in his hand. He glances casually around the room. He seems ready to leave when he suddenly notices* ELLEN, *who is still looking in the mirror with her back to him. He eyes her a moment, scratches his head, then quietly walks back toward her.*

CHARLEY: Well! It's a strange person who can behold a sight like that and *cry*! Or are they Narcissus tears of joy?

At the sound of his voice ELLEN *whirls about. She stares silently as he lights his cigarette.*

CHARLEY: Oh, forgive me! Won't you have one? *[Hastily produces a pack of cigarettes, which he holds out to her.]*

ELLEN: What are you doing here? *[Ignores cigarettes.]*

CHARLEY: The same thing you are, Ellen – looking at a beautiful woman! *[Returns cigarettes to his pocket.]*

ELLEN: How do you know my name? I've never met you.

CHARLEY: Oh, I heard Ellen Harcourt was the loveliest young lady here tonight. It wasn't hard at all. *[Walks to center stage in front of the sofa and stands there with his back to her, eyeing everything around him critically.]* A perfectly beautiful house! *[Turns to face her and smiles gallantly.]* A fitting abode for a creature as lovely as you, if I may say so.

ELLEN: How did you get here? *[Remains back by the mirror, watching him coldly.]*

CHARLEY: I was invited, oddly enough. I'm sorry I was too late for dinner, but it couldn't have been helped. Yes, I was invited, all right. I believe the person responsible was your eminent father.

ELLEN, *tartly:* Without my knowledge, of course.

CHARLEY: Of course! Your father must ask a number of people without his *own* knowledge – but such is the fate of senators.

ELLEN, *angrily:* I'll not have you insult my father!

CHARLEY: Certainly not! You mistake me. I daresay *all* fathers who give parties for their daughters find themselves in the same situation. – *All* fathers!

ELLEN: Why, how do *you* know? Are you married?

CHARLEY: Er – no. No, not at all. But my mother and father were.

ELLEN, *coming downstage left:* Really? I hadn't noticed.

CHARLEY, *grinning:* The lady has wit! You should go a long way, Ellen.

ELLEN: I'm beginning to think *you* should, too.

CHARLEY: Ah! A note of sarcasm! Are you asking me to leave?

ELLEN, *turning away:* Do as you like. I suppose, if Father asked you to come, you can stay until *he* asks you to leave – or until there's no excuse to stay.

CHARLEY: Meaning the end of the party?

ELLEN: If you will.

CHARLEY: But I don't! You've given me reason to stay forever. To look at you would make a man travel 'round the world, much less detain one already here!

ELLEN, *turning on him suddenly:* Well, that's all very nice, but I intend to go to bed tonight.

CHARLEY: Well, hooray! So do I!

ELLEN: I beg your pardon!

CHARLEY: Well, I should think you would! I'm sure Idi Amin and Princess Margaret plan to go to bed tonight – though not in the same bed, I trust.

ELLEN, *laughing in spite of herself:* I've never in my life –! You really are ridiculous!

CHARLEY, *triumphantly:* There! I've made you laugh, which was what I determined to do when I first caught sight of you. No matter the means! I have invoked laughter where tears used to be. My evening is a success!

ELLEN: You're high as a kite!

CHARLEY: I think so. Why?

ELLEN, *laughing again:* You're awfully funny! What's your name?

CHARLEY: Charley. Charles Herbert Morton, the Fourth, to be exact.

ELLEN: Well, Well! *[Points at him mockingly.]* You don't mean *this* has happened three times already!

CHARLEY: Oh, they had to perfect the model, you know.

ELLEN: You don't say! Well, won't you sit down, Charley —er, Charles Herbert Morton, the Fourth?

CHARLEY: Delighted! But if your other guests come in here to lynch me, remember – this was your idea. *[Sits down on sofa.]*

ELLEN, *sitting down beside him:* Oh, don't worry about *them.* I'm disgusted with it all, myself. Parties bore me to death. Don't all those people bore you, too? They must, or you wouldn't be here now!

CHARLEY: Well, I don't think they're all so bad – though I admit the company in here is better. On the other hand, the whiskey's better out there.

ELLEN, *laughing:* And without *that* you couldn't get through the party! Oh, no, you're not bored at all.

CHARLEY: Don't get me wrong! I enjoy meeting people at parties. Each new personality is a new experience – and all that! *[Laughs.]* As a matter of fact, I met an old college friend tonight whom I haven't seen in four years. Ha, ha, ha! And I wouldn't have missed seeing *him* for anything!

ELLEN: What are you laughing at?

CHARLEY: Oh, nothing. You wouldn't understand – I hope! Er, when you get right down to it, I don't go to parties very often. Don't have time for it. But if they're all as nice as this one, I wouldn't mind making a habit of it. *[Looks at Ellen and places his hand over hers, where it lies on the sofa between them.]*

ELLEN, *getting up and walking to the table at the end of the sofa, where she picks up a cigarette:* Oh, Father always does things up brown.
CHARLEY, *eyeing her with obvious approval:* Yes, I must say your father does things up brown. *[Gets up to light her cigarette.]*
ELLEN, *after getting her cigarette lit and walking away from him to the mantlepiece:* I was referring to the party tonight. I think your remark is hardly a compliment.
CHARLEY: I meant it as a compliment to your father, my dear – the gentleman who, if I'm not mistaken, is responsible for *both* of the parties in question.
ELLEN: I think we'd better change the subject.
CHARLEY, *walking to her and taking her hand in his:* By all means.
ELLEN, *withdrawing her hand:* That's not changing the subject.
CHARLEY: It's changing the subject of my compliments.
ELLEN, *laughing and walking a few steps left, away from him:* Do you know – if it weren't that you seem to have nice manners – I would suspect you of having designs on me?
CHARLEY: My dear girl – if it weren't for my being much addled by your father's liquor – you would be quite right.
ELLEN, *with a nervous little laugh:* You're awful! But I like you.
CHARLEY, *walking over to the mantlepiece, where he turns and looks back at her:* Well – since in life we must accept the bitter with the sweet, I accept the *kind* part of that and will do my best to forget the other – as I've been trying to do, these twenty-five years.
ELLEN: And has it been that difficult?
CHARLEY: Until tonight it's been almost impossible.
ELLEN: But tonight you find it easier?
CHARLEY: Tonight it's twice as hard. It's just that I find it

infinitely more worthwhile. *[Puts out his cigarette in an ashtray on the mantlepiece.]*

ELLEN, *pouting:* You *are* perfectly awful.

CHARLEY: But you like me!

ELLEN, *turning away from him:* I'm not sure I do. You make the most ungracious "compliments"! I don't know how to take them.

CHARLEY: But it means something that you take them at all.

ELLEN, *turning to face him:* But you realize I don't *have* to?

CHARLEY, *grinning:* However, you *are* taking them – and doing a very good job of it, too!

ELLEN, *walking slowly but firmly toward him:* Do you know – if you weren't tight – I should leave you this instant?

CHARLEY: Do you know, if I were sober, I should not have come in here in the first place?

ELLEN *draws back her hand and makes a feint, as if to slap him.*

CHARLEY, *laughing at her without moving:* Ha, ha, ha! You thought I was going to flinch, didn't you?

ELLEN: Ha, ha, ha! Yes! *[Slaps him, hard.]*

CHARLEY *stops laughing abruptly, raises his hand to his cheek a moment, then grabs* ELLEN *by the shoulders and kisses her in spite of her struggles.* ELLEN *finally breaks away and tries to slap him again. He catches her wrists and holds them.*

ELLEN, *struggling to free her hands:* Oh, you're the most awful person I've ever met in my life! Let me go!

CHARLEY, *smiling:* But you slapped me, without the usual provocation. If I'm going to be slapped, I'm going to deserve it.

ELLEN, *angrily:* You've *said* enough to be slapped a hundred times over!

CHARLEY, *with a silly grin: All* over?

ELLEN, *starting to struggle again:* Oh! My father will thrash you for insulting me! Let go! You're the most horrid person I've ever known! Let me go!

CHARLEY, *being serious:* In that case, I'm really sorry. I apologize, most humbly. *[Raises both her hands to his lips and kisses them.]*

ELLEN, *withdrawing her hands and turning away:* I think I'd better join the party. My father will wonder where I am.

CHARLEY, *taking a step toward her:* Oh, please don't go. I promise to behave like a gentleman from now on.

ELLEN, *walking slowly toward door, left:* Oh, it isn't that.

CHARLEY: Then I'll promise *not* to behave like a gentleman.

ELLEN, *turning toward him as she reaches the doorway:* You're really impossible! I must get back to my party. After all, it's only being given in my honor, and –

She is interrupted by SENATOR HARCOURT, *who thrusts himself through the door, left, laughing loudly. He is almost sixty years old, very fat, and red-faced. He wears a black tuxedo and a paper party-hat with long plumes.*

SENATOR HARCOURT, *almost knocking* ELLEN *down*: Oh, there you are, Daughter! I've been looking for you. Want to introduce you to Dr. Morton. I knew his mother and father before they knew each other, and – *[Sees* CHARLEY.*]* Well, *Charley*, you young rapscallion, you! *[Goes to* CHARLEY *and slaps him heavily on the back.]* Your old man never used to wait for introductions, either! Ha, ha, ha! I guess that's how he got to be such a good travelling salesman, eh? Ha, ha, ha! *[Nudges* CHARLEY *in the ribs.]*

ELLEN: Father, please! Dr. Morton and I have hardly met! We were just –

CHARLEY: Er – yes, we were just going to look for you, Senator, to make it official.

SENATOR HARCOURT: Ha, ha, ha! *[Slaps him on the back again.]* That's hardly necessary, my boy! Any son of old "Rocky" Charley Morton is a son of mi – er – needs no introduction!

CHARLEY: Well, thank you very much, sir.

SENATOR HARCOURT: Yes, I certainly am glad you met my daughter, Charley. I've been wanting to get you two together for a long time. They don't come any better than your old man. Now that you know where we live, I hope you'll make yourself at home here whenever you like. Yes, sir! And to start things off right, why don't we have our own little party in here? We can begin by drinking a toast to Ellen on the spot!

CHARLEY: Wonderful idea!

ELLEN: Father! We'd better get back to the drawingroom – your other guests. Besides, we haven't anything to drink a toast *with* in here.

SENATOR HARCOURT: Oh, ho, *ho!* That's what you and your mother think! *[Takes a few mincing steps over to bookcase, right, humming and rubbing his hands together. Stops in front of bookcase, scanning the shelves.]* Let me see, now. What was – oh, yes! *Memoirs of Ulysses S. Grant! [Takes down a volume from the bookcase, reaches in behind it, and pulls out a half-full quart of whiskey with an inverted glass on top of it.]* Ah, here we are. *[Looks at bottle fondly.]* My very best private stock – only for rare, rare occasions. *[Goes over to* CHARLEY *and* ELLEN, *who have remained motionless, watching him.]* You know, this stuff is damn' well older than I am. Think of it! Before I was even born, some Scotchman made this for me. Mighty decent of him. And people ask me why I vote to send money to Britain! Damn' well wish I could send 'em *myself!*

ELLEN: Thank you very much, Father, but Dr. Morton and I–

CHARLEY, *interrupting:* Why, yes, indeed, sir! We'd love to have a drink! *[Moves a step away from* SENATOR HARCOURT *in anticipation of being slapped on the back again.]*

SENATOR HARCOURT, *reaching out and placing a hand on* CHARLEY'S *shoulder:* Spoke' like a true son of "Rocky" Charley, my boy! Ha, ha, ha! How 'bout it, Ellen – a short one for you?

ELLEN: Thank you Father. You *know* I don't drink.

SENATOR HARCOURT: Oh, come on Ellen. You're big enough to stop kidding your old man. Your mother's not around! If you promise not to tell on me, why, I'll forget I saw *you* this once!

ELLEN: I don't care for any Father! And I shouldn't think you would, either.

SENATOR HARCOURT: Oh, come on, Ellen! Tell you what I'll do. Since we don't have but one glass, we'll all three drink out of the bottle. That way, I won't know how much you take. *[Sets glass on table at left of sofa.]*

ELLEN, *emphatically:* No, thank you!

SENATOR HARCOURT: Well, if you won't drink to yourself, I bet Dr. Morton will. Never knew a doctor who didn't drink when he wasn't operating. – Matter of fact, from the way my liver's been acting up since I had it fixed, I'd say some of 'em drink even while they *are* operating.

CHARLEY, *looking at the bottle longingly:* I believe I'd drink to your daughter under any circumstances, Senator.

SENATOR HARCOURT, *beaming:* And I couldn't blame you, son. Er – let me try this stuff and see whether it's still all right. *[Takes top off bottle and has a generous drink.]* Seems all right. Well, Daughter, here's looking at me! *[Takes another pull at the bottle.]*

ELLEN: Father! *[Tugging at his arm.]*

SENATOR HARCOURT, *swallowing hard with both eyes shut, then opening them and looking around quickly:* What? Huh? What's the matter?

ELLEN, *reaching for the bottle:* Father! You're embarrassing me!

SENATOR HARCOURT, *keeping the bottle beyond her reach:* Dammit, girl! It's bad enough to be hen-pecked. But, by God, I draw the line at being *pullet*-pecked!

ELLEN: Father, really! Remember you have to make a speech in the Senate tomorrow morning.

SENATOR HARCOURT: Who, me? Make speech in the Senate? – My God! You're right! *[Takes another drink from the bottle.]*

MRS. HARCOURT, *entering door, left, while the Senator is still drinking:* Harvey! Harvey, give me that thing this instant! *[Snatches bottle from him as he stands with his empty hand still extended, mouth full, cheeks puffed out.]* You are certainly the limit! I've been looking all over this house for you. *[Puts bottle down on table at left of sofa.]* There's a very important 'phone call waiting for you and a house full of people – and here you stand like a perfect fool, not caring a thing about your guests!

SENATOR HARCOURT, *swallowing hard:* But, Aggie – we were having our own little party here.

MRS. HARCOURT: Well, suppose you take care of the party on the 'phone. Then you come with me and stop acting this way. *[Takes his arm and pulls him over to the table, downstage right of fireplace. Hands him the telephone receiver as* ELLEN *starts toward door, left, followed by* CHARLEY.*]*

SENATOR HARCOURT, *seeing them about to leave:* Oh, don't go away, Ellen – Charley. This won't take a minute. *[Into the 'phone.]* Hello? Hello . . .? No, I don't know anybody by that name. *[Drops receiver and starts to walk across to his bottle, but* MRS. HARCOURT *jerks him back.]*

MRS. HARCOURT: Harvey Harcourt! If you don't behave, I'm going to make your head look like a beaten biscuit! Now, pick up that 'phone and talk!

SENATOR HARCOURT: All right, Aggie, all right! You don't have to get fractious about it! *[Reels in the 'phone cord till he gets the receiver in his hands.]* Hello? . . . Yes, this is Senator Harcourt. Who's that? . . . Oh, *Jimmy!* For Pete's sake, you didn't have to call me! . . . Well, I'm sorry you couldn't make it, myself. . . . Yeah, well don't feel too bad—we're having a hell of a time without you . . . . Oh, I understand. Elections, like the poor, are always with us . . . . Sure. Well, I wouldn't let *that* worry me. Elephants will still eat peanuts, even if people won't. . . . Yeah, I sure will . . . . And, Jimmy – don't take any wooden nominations! Ha, ha, ha! 'Bye. *[Hangs up 'phone.]*

MRS. HARCOURT: All right. Now, if you'll just come with me, Mrs. Fitzsimmons wants you to tell her about the African situation.

SENATOR HARCOURT: Mrs. Fitzsimmons? Aw, Aggie, I can't tell *her* anything. She ought to go the hell over there herself. – And I haven't seen Charley Morton in–

MRS. HARCOURT: Yes, I know. You haven't seen him since he was knee-high to a pink elephant. But you *must* get back to your party! *[Begins pulling him toward door, left.]*

SENATOR HARCOURT: Now, wait a minute, Aggie. You remember what your old friend "Grinch" Gibson told me, don't you? He said to me, he said, "Harvey, you old son of a gun – you throw the best parties in Washington, and then you spoil 'em all by coming to 'em yourself!"

MRS. HARCOURT, *trying to guide him through the door:* That's all very true. But Mr. Gibson isn't here tonight, and perhaps every one else isn't so particular.

SENATOR HARCOURT: Wait, wait a minute, Aggie. I have to tell Charley something! *[She stops momentarily.]* Charley – something I want you to tell your old man the next time you see him. Did you hear the one about the two old maids and the Siamese twins? Well, there were these two old maids, see, and one of 'em was a trifle deaf, and . . . *[Goes off through door, left, shoved by his wife.]*

MRS. HARCOURT, *re-entering for a moment and turning to* ELLEN: I know how you must feel, dear! Don't bother to come back to the party. You must be terribly upset! And don't worry about your father. I'll take care of *him*! *[Goes back off left before* ELLEN *can answer.]*

ELLEN *turns away from the door and goes to the sofa. She plumps herself down, looking completely disgusted.* CHARLEY, *standing to the left, smiles to himself.*

CHARLEY: Well, it seems we're having romantic problems.

ELLEN: That's *my* business.

CHARLEY: And that of whoever loves you.

ELLEN: I'd rather not discuss it.

CHARLEY: Well, a girl like you must have lots of men crazy about her – and I suppose that *does* lead to trouble. But you wouldn't be happy if you didn't have people asking you to marry them all the time, would you?

ELLEN, *emphatically:* I'd rather not discuss it.

CHARLEY, *frowning:* Yes, I guess that's why you wanted to get away from *me* just now – I hadn't asked you to marry me.

ELLEN, *angrily:* I said I'd rather not discuss it!

CHARLEY, *walking over to the sofa:* All right, Ellen. I just thought that, since we have now been formally introduced, we could talk a little more politely.

ELLEN, *not looking at him but folding her arms stiffly:* Speak for yourself.

CHARLEY: Oh, I intend to! *[Picks up bottle and glass from the table.]* Er – would you like a drink?

ELLEN: You heard me tell my father I don't drink.

CHARLEY: But I'm not your father.

ELLEN, *looking at him suddenly:* You don't say! In that case, I think I will.

They both laugh. CHARLEY *pours her a small drink and hands it to her. She gulps it down, chokes, and coughs violently.*

CHARLEY, *laughing:* Your first? *[Takes glass from her.]*

ELLEN: Close to it. I rarely indulge. I just thought it might do me some good tonight.

CHARLEY, *pouring himself a more generous drink:* Has the evening really been that bad?

ELLEN: Yes! And it's not over yet.

CHARLEY: Meaning – me?

ELLEN: Meaning you.

He sits down beside her, but she turns away.

CHARLEY: I apologized once. I'll do it again, if it'll help. – I'm sorry if I hurt your feelings. Did I hurt them that badly?

ELLEN, *getting up and walking over to the mantlepiece, where she stands with her back to him:* You're a doctor. You should know about affairs of the heart better than I.

CHARLEY: Oh, that "doctor" business! It's a joke of your father's. I'm only in my senior year at medical school, on the way to becoming a psychiatrist. I still have much to learn. As a matter of fact, I ought to be studying *now.*

ELLEN *whirls around indignantly. As soon as she turns,* CHARLEY *looks down at his glass and takes a drink from it.*

ELLEN, *walking across stage to the left, her back to him:* Well, I'd consider your apology much more genuine if you would stop drinking and behave yourself.

He looks first at the glass, then at her, and finally downs his drink at a gulp.

CHARLEY: You're right. Not another drop tonight! – You know – it's funny – *life* is, in a way, like one big drink of whiskey.

ELLEN, *turning to face him:* What do you mean? You can never get enough of it?

CHARLEY: That's not what I had in mind, but you may have something there! – No, what I mean is, you have to guard against too much of life, the same way you have to be careful you don't get too much whiskey at one time.

ELLEN: And what could that mean, coming from you?

CHARLEY: You have to protect yourself from too much reality. Some people do it by never taking anything seriously. But that's the same thing as never taking a sip out of your "one big drink of whiskey"! Some people don't guard against life at all. They take it *so* seriously – try to do so *much* all the time – that they just crack up completely. Er – they are the ones who try to take their whole drink at once. The best way is to work hard while you're working and relax hard while you're playing. Take life the way you ought to take whiskey – in little amounts, spread far enough apart so the separate bits can't gang up on you. You follow me?

ELLEN: I'm not sure.

CHARLEY: Well, it's just a question of finding something you can lose yourself in besides your primary interest in life –like taking a chaser between straight shots. Remember you'll have to put your drink down once in a while, unless you want to be like the people who try to take it all at once. Don't be afraid to share your drink with somebody else, and above all! – never turn down a taste of somebody else's when it's offered. Simple!

ELLEN: And do you live by your own prescription?

CHARLEY: Of course! I'm in the "work-hard, play-hard" category. It's the only way.

ELLEN: Do you *work* hard?

CHARLEY: Do I work *hard?* Does a hippopotamus have hips?

ELLEN, *walking across to right of sofa:* And where do *I* fit into your "life-is-one-big-drink-of-whiskey" theory?

CHARLEY: Why, you haven't even poured yours out of the bottle!

ELLEN: What do you mean by that?

CHARLEY: You haven't begun to live! You've seen only one side of life – the top side, granted – but too much candy will make a *dog* sick. – I could tell right away that you're bored. I knew you didn't want to go back to the party in there, even when you pretended to. – You've never found out what life is like! If you had, you'd know how well off you are. I'm not saying this kind of life – parties and all that – is the ideal way to spend your time. *[Glances at* SENATOR HARCOURT'S *bottle.]* But it has its aspects – in addition to eighty-year old Scotch! In short – you ought to know something of hell before you start judging heaven!

ELLEN, *coldly:* Thank you, Doctor! Are you going to charge me for the advice?

CHARLEY: Not at all. It's just that I'd like to see such a lovely butterfly break out of her cocoon.

ELLEN: And do you think *you* have?

CHARLEY: That's rather a false question. *I'm* not a lovely butterfly. However, I *am* farther along than you – and that's all that matters.

ELLEN: I fail to see how it matters at all.

CHARLEY: Well, as your husband, I'll be able to help you along. And as Granddaddy used to tell Grandma, "I can draw inspiration from your youthful candor and refreshing innocence."

ELLEN, *aghast:* "As your husband"– !

CHARLEY: Well, you would have to be *my wife.* You see–

ELLEN: Why, Charley Morton! Are you proposing to me?

CHARLEY, *getting up from sofa and walking left:* You know, I hate that word "propose." It sounds so – so Victorian and "one-knee-on-the-floor"-ish. Life's too short for that sort of thing. – But you've got the idea. If you'll marry me, I'd be much obliged.

ELLEN, *incredulous:* You're asking me to *marry* you?

CHARLEY: Well, you said you'd rather not discuss it. I didn't know exactly how to put it.

ELLEN: Well, never in my life –! Why, you must be the most idiotic, the most conceited –!

CHARLEY, *interrupting:* That's quite possible. But will you marry me?

ELLEN: You don't even know me! How on earth can you ask me to marry you?

CHARLEY, *walking toward her:* My dear Ellen, you do me a great injustice. I know that you must be good at tennis and swimming, and that you like such things as music and art and literature. *[Turning front and scratching his head.]* The only thing you'll have to get used to is being a doctor's wife.

ELLEN: We've only just *met.* How can you claim to know such things about me?

CHARLEY: It's really not hard. I gathered from Brad Hemmings–

ELLEN, *furious:* Brad Hemmings! How dare you– !

CHARLEY: Now, don't get me wrong! So help me heaven, the only thing he told me about you was – and I quote – "Goddammit, she wouldn't marry me!" And I hadn't even asked him for that. You see, Brad and I went to college together. He's the old friend I told you I'd met tonight. I was really glad to see him. Funny fellow, though. Pretty conceited. Hadn't much upstairs, but he was a hell of an athlete. I guessed you must like his sports or he wouldn't have been interested in you. And since you refused him, I thought you must be some sort of intellectual – or at least think you are. *[At this she turns her back on him.]* Oh – and he *did* give me one other piece of information – not that I really needed it! He said you were the prettiest girl at the party. Old Brad always knew how to pick 'em!

ELLEN, *turning on him suddenly:* Very clever, Mr. Sherlock Holmes! But you can't expect me to take your proposal seriously.

CHARLEY: Why the hell not? You think I'm kidding?

ELLEN, *turning and walking away from him:* I think you're crazy.

CHARLEY, *following her:* You could have it annulled, if it turns out I was crazy beforehand.

ELLEN, *facing him suddenly:* Have you ever heard of the word "love"? It so happens that it's very important to a marriage, and you haven't mentioned it once. At least Brad Hemmings *loved* me when he asked me to marry *him!* But *you— oh* no! It's like buying a new car, or something! *[Turns and walks back toward the French windows.]*

CHARLEY, *as if to himself:* "Love"? I never thought of that! *[Louder, to* ELLEN.*]* Well, Ellen, that goes without saying. I wouldn't ask some one to marry me if I didn't love her. I thought you'd know that.

ELLEN, *facing him again:* Well! That's about the most romantic way of putting it I ever heard! What do you think I am — some harem girl you can treat any way you like? Being married to you would be like living with a clown. You're not only crazy — you're drunk! And if there's anything I hate, it's crazy people who're drunk. *[Turns and walks around in front of sofa.]*

CHARLEY, *following her:* But, Ellen — I loved you from the first minute I laid eyes on you. — In fact, even before that. It was as soon as I heard Brad Hemmings say, "Goddammit, she wouldn't marry me!" — If you'd just hold still, I'd kiss you and prove it!

ELLEN, *moving off: Oh!* Get away from me!

CHARLEY: Well, I admit it's a bit sudden and all that. But I thought, since you'd already had one person ask you to marry him tonight, you'd be all set for the next.

ELLEN, *going to table and picking up whiskey bottle:* I wish I knew just how drunk you are! Because if you aren't drunker than you've ever been in your life, I ought to break this over your head.

CHARLEY, *sounding serious:* Oh, Ellen, I'm cold sober — by now! But I never intended to *insult* you. — It's just that — well, you're the first girl I ever asked to marry me.

ELLEN, *putting down bottle:* Well, I hope you've learned something. I have a feeling you'll be doing it pretty often before you get a wife.

CHARLEY: Oh, Ellen, you just don't understand. With all the work I have to do in medical school, I don't have time to waste on girls. If you won't marry me, I'll just have to say goodbye – try to forget you, some way or other. Honestly, you have no idea what the work is like. I can't afford to worry about things like this. The pressure's on me twenty-four hours a day. *[Moves closer to her.]* But I – I *do* want you to know that I love you. And I want you to be my wife. Ellen – Ellen, I've never in my life asked another girl to marry me. I've never *wanted* another girl to marry me.

ELLEN, *more tenderly:* Well, thank you, Charley.

CHARLEY: You mean – you mean, you consider it a compliment?

ELLEN: I'd consider it the nicest I've ever had – if I could believe it.

CHARLEY, *taking her hands in his:* Ellen! You *must* believe it! Ellen, look at me! *[She looks up into his eyes.]* Why? Why won't you believe me?

ELLEN, *falteringly:* You're a fascinating person, Charley. – But I don't know whether to believe *anything* you tell me.

CHARLEY: Ellen, please! I'm not joking and I'm not drunk! Can't you understand that I love you?

ELLEN, *softly:* No, Charley, I can't.

CHARLEY: Ellen, please. Whether you marry me or not is *one* thing. But I want you to know that I *love* you. Will you believe that?

ELLEN, *softly, looking into his eyes:* Oh, Charley – if I believed that, I would have to marry you!

CHARLEY: Ellen, can't I make you understand? Don't you know you're beautiful enough to make a man fall in love with you the first time he sees you? *[She does not answer.]* Ellen! *[Tries to kiss her.]*

ELLEN, *moving away:* No, Charley, don't. I only know that you couldn't mean it. It's impossible that you should be in love with me! *[Goes to the mantlepiece and remains there with her back to him.]*

CHARLEY: Isn't there *anything* I can do to make you believe me?

ELLEN, *almost crying, hiding her face in her hands:* No! Nothing!

CHARLEY: Then I'll say goodbye, Ellen. I must have been a fool even to look at you. I'll never be able to forget this. But I won't trouble you again.

CHARLEY *turns and starts to leave, going around the table by the sofa toward the French windows.* ELLEN *begins to cry softly. He catches sight of the whiskey bottle, which is still standing on the end table. He picks it up and looks at it.*

CHARLEY: Whiskey! If it hadn't been for this, you would have believed me!

He glances at ELLEN *and then raises the bottle as if to smash it on the floor. Suddenly he stops. He pulls a half-pint bottle out of his coat pocket. He compares the two, tucks* SENATOR HARCOURT'S *bottle under his coat, and dashes the half-pint down on the floor, where it breaks with a crash. Then he runs out through the French windows.*

ELLEN *looks up and turns quickly at the sound of the breaking glass. She runs around the sofa, glances down at the smashed bottle, and then runs out through the French windows.*

ELLEN, *on the terrace:* Charley! Charley!

MRS. HARCOURT, *entering hurriedly from the door, left, and looking round the room:* Ellen! Ellen, what's the matter? Where are you? Ellen?

ELLEN, *running in from the terrace, crying:* Oh, Mother, he's gone! And he was perfectly violent when he left! I don't know *what* he's going to do!

MRS. HARCOURT, *putting her arm around* ELLEN: There, there, child. What's the matter? What happened?

ELLEN, *still sobbing:* He asked me to marry him – and when I said I wouldn't, he smashed Father's bottle and left in an awful rage!

MRS. HARCOURT: There, there, now, Ellen! Don't worry about it. Your father has plenty of bottles. – Who did all this? Brad?

ELLEN, *twisting away from her:* Oh, Brad hasn't the wit to do anything, Mother! It was Charley Morton!

MRS. HARCOURT: What! You mean Charley Morton asked you to marry him? That's ridiculous. He'd only just met you.

ELLEN, *testily:* Well, what's ridiculous about that? I thought he was a charming person.

MRS. HARCOURT: Nothing, nothing, my dear. – His father was a bit peculiar on the subject of women, too!

ELLEN, *angrily:* He is *not* peculiar! He wanted me to marry him! And when I wouldn't, he left here as though he were going to kill himself!

MRS. HARCOURT: There, there, dear! You've had a very strenuous evening. You go along to bed now, and I'll come see you when I can get free. The party's almost over, and your father has quieted nicely.

ELLEN, *longingly:* But, Mother, he was the only person who I – who ever really interested me! And now he's gone and I'll never see him again!

MRS. HARCOURT: Now, now, Ellen, don't worry about it. I felt the same way when I refused your father the first time. I thought I would never see *him* again – but was *I* fooled!

ELLEN: Oh, but, Mother, you don't understand! Charley loves me, and he thinks I don't believe him!

MRS. HARCOURT: Well, that's nothing to cry about. You don't, do you?

ELLEN: I – I don't know. I'm so completely mixed up.

MRS. HARCOURT: Well, then, it's a good thing he left. It'll give you some time to think. – Heavenly days, but this room smells of whiskey! Has your father been back in here?

ELLEN, *impatiently:* No, Mother, that was Charley. I told you, he broke Father's bottle.

MRS. HARCOURT: Do you mean to tell me – Charley Morton's boy broke a bottle with whiskey in it? – on *purpose?*
ELLEN: Oh, Mother, you don't understand at all! He did it because he was so upset when I told him I thought he was drunk.
MRS. HARCOURT, *going toward door, left:* Well, if you thought he was drunk, he probably was. Any daughter of Harvey Harcourt ought to know when a man is drunk! – But go along to bed now. I'll be up in a moment to see you.
ELLEN, *following her slowly:* But, Mother – do you think he'll ever come back?
MRS. HARCOURT: Oh, yes, indeed, he'll come back. If he asked you to marry him after just meeting you, he's liable to do anything!
ELLEN, *turning toward the French windows:* Oh, Mother! You're not being helpful at all!
MRS. HARCOURT, *going to her daughter and putting an arm around her:* Well, come on to bed and don't think about it any more. If we're not dead, we'll all feel better in the morning.
She leads ELLEN *gently through the door, left. The stage darkens to indicate the passage of several hours.*
When the stage lights come up again, it is morning. Sunlight streams through the open French windows. Sounds of singing birds float in from the terrace.
ELLEN *enters from door, left. She is still wearing her evening dress, which looks as though she had slept in it. She walks slowly across to the French windows, stands there a moment looking out, then turns and walks back around the sofa to the table. She stands looking down at the place where* CHARLEY *smashed his bottle. She stoops and picks up a piece of broken glass. She holds it in her hand as she looks again toward the French windows. At last she puts the piece of glass on the end-table and walks across to the mantlepiece, where she begins to cry softly.*

CHARLEY *suddenly appears outside on the terrace. His collar is open, his tuxedo wrinkled, his hair thoroughly messed. He walks silently into the room and stands behind the sofa with a strange half-smile on his face. He remains there without moving, watching* ELLEN.

ELLEN, *turning at last to go across to the door left, and seeing him:* Oh! Charley! *[She starts back at first.]* You frightened me. Oh, but I'm so glad to see you! I was perfectly frantic when you left like that last night. I haven't slept a wink!

CHARLEY, *staring at her:* Oh, Ellen, I knew you loved me. I might have *known* you wouldn't let me do it. I must have been crazy. Will you ever forgive me?

ELLEN: Why, Charley, what do you mean? What's wrong?

CHARLEY, *coming around the sofa unsteadily, never taking his eyes from her face:* When you met me on the bridge a while ago – you didn't know it, but I was going to throw myself over! I've never in my life had trouble forgetting any one – but I knew I could never forget you. I'd been walking all night. I decided to kill myself.

ELLEN, *taking a step toward him, putting her hands up to her cheeks:* Oh, Charley, Charley! No!

CHARLEY, *as if he had not heard:* Then all of a sudden I was on that bridge – with the river there, so close to me, ready to wash away all thought of you!

ELLEN, *shaking her head:* Oh, no, no, it couldn't be – !

CHARLEY, *going on as before:* And then – I don't know how or why – I felt some one was standing there with me. I turned, and there you were – smiling – still wearing that white dress– looking even more beautiful than I remembered.

ELLEN, *going to him and putting her hands on his arms:* Oh, Charley, Charley! No! It's not true!

CHARLEY, *looking down at her:* You said, "I thought I had lost you!" Then you walked right up and kissed me. I closed my eyes – and when I looked again, you'd gone. I was all alone. Oh,

Ellen, you didn't know what you'd saved me from! But as soon as I saw you there, I knew you loved me! I only wondered whether I could go back to you after – after almost doing something so – so unworthy of you.

ELLEN: Charley, don't, don't – !

CHARLEY: But I felt I *must*. – I had to see you – ask you to forgive me for being such a fool.

ELLEN: Charley, don't! You don't have to. I love you, Charley! I love you! *[Embraces him.]*

CHARLEY, *motionless in her embrace:* But, Ellen, it was so awful! – And if you hadn't come to me, I would never have seen you again. I would never have known you loved me.

ELLEN, *frantically, her arms around him:* Yes, but you know it now! Forget what happened out there last night. Just remember I love you and never think about what happened on any bridge. *Promise* me you'll never think about it again!

CHARLEY: Will you marry me if I promise?

ELLEN: Oh, yes, yes, a thousand times *yes!* Only promise me you'll never think about – about *that* again!

CHARLEY: I'll promise anything in the world you want. *[Kisses her lightly.]*

ELLEN, *standing back from him with her hands on his arms:* But, Charley – there's something I must tell you – now that you've promised to forget that awful business on the bridge.

CHARLEY: Yes, dearest, what is it?

ELLEN: You promise you'll forget it forever?

CHARLEY: I told you I'd promise anything you want.

ELLEN: Then, Charley, you must know that – that I haven't been out of the house all evening! Honestly, darling, I haven't! I was lying awake in my room till just a few minutes ago. But I *haven't been out of the house*!

CHARLEY *looks at her seriously for a moment. He stands without saying a word, then breaks slowly into a smile.*

CHARLEY: I think I should tell you something – if you promise to forget it right away.

ELLEN, *moving close to him:* Certainly! I promise, Charley.

CHARLEY: You promise you'll forget it forever –?

ELLEN: Oh, *yes,* dearest! What is it?

CHARLEY: – that you'll never think about it again? – that you won't think the less of me for it?

ELLEN: Oh yes! Yes, I do!

CHARLEY: Well, you said you hadn't been out of the house all night –

ELLEN, *earnestly:* Yes, darling. I'm sorry, but I swear I haven't!

CHARLEY, *taking* ELLEN'S *hands in his:* Well, Ellen, you dearest, loveliest thing in the world – *neither have I* – but I love you!

ELLEN *blushes crimson. She starts to say something, stops, looks hard at him, and then with a laugh throws her arms around his neck. They both laugh as they hold each other. Then* CHARLEY *kisses her. As the curtain begins to come slowly down, he opens one eye and winks at the audience without breaking the kiss.*

The curtain falls on their embrace.

FOR THEY SHALL SEE GOD

A Play in One Act

THE CHARACTERS

GEORGE HARRISON, a businessman

HELEN HARRISON, his wife

JIM HARRISON, his son

HENRY HILL, the butler

MAGGIE JONES, the cook

DR. JOHN BERKELEY, a guest

A FIGURE IN BLACK

FOR THEY SHALL SEE GOD

Scene: The diningroom of GEORGE HARRISON'S *home in Richmond, Virginia.*
Time: An evening in 1952, a few minutes before dinner. The stage darkens once to denote the passage of approximately two hours.

The curtain rises on the diningroom of a well-to-do Southern family. The table is downstage right. A handsome sideboard stands against the wall, left. At the rear of the room and right of center a wide double doorway leads into the front hall of the house. The front door is just visible through this doorway at extreme backstage right. The hall leads off backstage left into the rest of the house. At the rear of the room and left of center a swinging door leads off to the pantry and the kitchen. The room is tastefully furnished. Several chairs (matching those at the table) stand about the room. Hunting prints and one or two oil portraits hang on the walls. Windows in the right and left walls face each other behind drawn curtains. The table is set for dinner with four places, one on each side.
MRS. HARRISON *enters suddenly from the hall. She is past middle-age but still quite attractive.*
MRS. HARRISON, *anxiously:* Henry! Henry! Good heavens, Henry! Something terrible has happened. – There wasn't a thing I could do about it! Not one thing!
As she speaks, MR. HARRISON *enters from the hall, holding an open newspaper. He is several years older and a bit heavier than his wife.* HENRY, *the Negro butler, enters from the pantry as* MR. HARRISON *comes in from the hall.* HENRY, *though apparently vigorous, is close to seventy years of age. He wears an old, but neatly pressed black suit and a black bowtie. His clothes*

are somewhat too big for him, but he looks very much at home in them.

MR. HARRISON: What on earth is the matter, Helen?

MRS. HARRISON: Oh, Dr. Berkeley just 'phoned to say an old friend from out of town had dropped in for a visit. He felt he would have to decline our dinner invitation – and then, of course, I had to invite them both.

MR. HARRISON, *mocking her:* And, of course, Dr. Berkeley had to *accept* for them both!

MRS. HARRISON: Exactly! John Berkeley makes me so mad I could scream. Calling just before dinner to bring another guest! He must think I run a hotel. Old bachelors who live by themselves are God's own trial of us all!

MR. HARRISON: You should save something to say about old bachelors who *don't* live by themselves.

MRS. HARRISON: George, it's not funny. You have no idea what it is to plan dinner and then have everything ruined at the last minute!

HENRY, *in the mild tone he generally uses:* Aw, dat's all right, Miz Harrison. We can fix up somethin' fo' one mo' gent'man. Don't you worry 'bout it, ma'am. Maggie an' me'll take care of ever'thing.

MRS. HARRISON: Well, thank you, Henry. I'm sorry this has to fall on you.

HENRY: Dat's all right, Miz Harrison. Whoever 'tis, we'll be ready fo' him when he come'. *[Goes out pantry door.]*

MRS. HARRISON: Honestly, George! Your friends! You'd think they wouldn't impose this way on *any*body, much less some one they care about.

MR. HARRISON: Well, whom else *can* they impose on, my dear? That's what friends are for! I'm *glad* he's bringing his guest. John Berkeley's one of my best and dearest. There's nothing he wouldn't do for me. *[Going toward her.]* Don't take on so, Helen. Henry said he could manage.

MRS. HARRISON: That's not the point, George. Henry's old. He hasn't been at all well lately. I don't like to put any more on him. You know he had that – that heart attack, or whatever it was, last week while you were away. He's still shaky from it. He wouldn't let a soul come near him – and I couldn't make him see a doctor.

MR. HARRISON: Yes, well, there's not much you can do about a bad heart, Helen. – It can't be serious, though. Henry's strong as a horse! – never been sick in his life!

MRS. HARRISON: I know, George, but he's almost seventy. At that age it means something to have a heart attack. The other day Maggie found him asleep at the kitchen table over his lunch. She says he talks to himself and stares at her sometimes till she's afraid to go near him.

MR. HARRISON: Oh, nonsense! Henry wouldn't hurt a soul! He's just getting old – like the rest of us. Nothing we can do about that.

MRS. HARRISON: Oh, George, you don't understand at all!

MR. HARRISON, *smiling:* Well, I invited Dr. Berkeley to dinner, dear! He *is* a heart specialist, you know.

MRS. HARRISON: How nice! Have you got an undertaker coming tomorrow?

MR. HARRISON: Helen, simmer down! I'll ask the good doctor to look at Henry after dinner, if you want. I know John wouldn't mind.

MRS. HARRISON: Yes, I *do* want! Henry troubles me terribly.

MR. HARRISON, *going to his wife and putting an arm around her:* I'll speak to John. Don't worry. [HENRY *re-enters from the pantry with silverware, napkin, glasses, etc., for another place at the table.* MR. HARRISON *drops his arm and walks back to the hall door, where he turns to his wife before leaving.]* Is there anything I can do to help? Oh, by the way, who's the extra guest?

MRS. HARRISON, *turning to help* HENRY *set the fifth place:* An old army friend of yours – Jerry Bingham.

MR. HARRISON, *thunderstruck:* Jerry Bingham?

MRS. HARRISON, *without looking up from the table:* That's right.

MR. HARRISON: Not "Brat" Bingham?

MRS. HARRISON, *coolly:* I've heard him called that.

MR. HARRISON, *throwing his newspaper on the floor:* Well, I'll be *damned!*

MRS. HARRISON: Suit yourself.

MR. HARRISON: Well, why didn't you say you couldn't have him? – make some kind of excuse? Tell John Berkeley –

MRS. HARRISON, *turning suddenly from the table:* That's right! Blame it on me! It's all *my* fault when one of your inconsiderate friends brings one more just like him to dinner!

MR. HARRISON, *hotly:* Jerry Bingham is no inconsiderate friend of mine! He's – he's no friend of mine at all! And what the devil John Berkeley means by bringing him here to dinner! *[Shakes his head.]* Berkeley hasn't the sense of a heathen horsefly!

HENRY: 'Scuse me, suh, but ain't dat de Mistah Bingham who was hyar on Christmas Day?

MR. HARRISON: Yes, by God, he *was* here Christmas! And once a year is *enough* for the likes of Bingham!

HENRY: Well, suh, it won't be no trouble to take care of Mistah Bingham. He don't mind if he eat or not, long as dere's liquor handy. An' you got plenty of whiskey in de basement closet, Mistah Harrison.

MRS. HARRISON, *looking hard at her husband:* Yes, I'm sure there's plenty of whiskey.

HENRY, *smiling and talking almost as if to himself:* One time when he was hyar, Mistah Bingham tol' me he could get plenty of food at home. *[Shakes his head.]* Say he didn' want none o' dat. But he say his wife wouldn' let him keep no liquor in de house, so he had to drink all he could hol' whenever he went out.

MR. HARRISON: Er, yes – well, er – I'll bring some more up. *[Goes out the door to the pantry.]*

MRS. HARRISON, *helping* HENRY *move another chair to the table*: Let's see, Henry. We'll put Mr. Bingham and Dr. Berkeley down at this end on either side of Mr. Harrison. Put Jim at my end next to Dr. Berkeley. It's just as well the other children won't be home for supper now.

HENRY: Yas, ma'am.

MRS. HARRISON: I declare, Henry, it certainly is a blessing *you* don't drink. You've no idea what a comfort it is to Mr. Harrison and me that you never have.

HENRY: Aw, I *use* to, Miz Harrison – fo' I come to work fo' y' all.

MRS. HARRISON: Oh, did you? I never knew! But I suppose you *must* have – or you wouldn't be able to mix drinks the way you do. How did you happen to give it up?

HENRY: Oh, de Lawd jes' tol' me I'd have to stop, Miz Harrison. Dey warn't nothin' else I could do.

MRS. HARRISON: Now, Henry! Was it the Lord or your father? I remember hearing old Luther Hill tell *me* a hundred times never to touch a drop of anything stronger than water.

HENRY, *smiling:* It might of been both, Miz Harrison!

MRS. HARRISON: Well, I wish the Lord would speak to a few people *I* could name!

JIM HARRISON, *yelling from upstairs: Mother!* What happened to that dress shirt I was going to wear to the party tonight?

MRS. HARRISON, *going to the hall doorway to answer:* It's in my room, Jim. I had Maggie restarch the front and press it for you this afternoon. You wrinkled it badly when you brought it home from college. Are you ready for it?

JIM: Am I ready? I've gone through every drawer in the place, looking for it! You can't lay anything down around here without having somebody tuck it away or send it out to the cleaner's! *[*MR. HARRISON, *with a bottle of whiskey, enters from the pantry while* JIM *is still yelling.]* It's enough to make me feel I'm *married* or something!

MR. and MRS. HARRISON, *to each other in shocked surprise:* "Or *something"?*

MR. HARRISON: I'll have to *speak* to that boy! – Do me a favor, dear: check to see that we have enough ice and glasses in the livingroom.

MRS. HARRISON: As soon as I've checked on "the shirtless wonder." *[Goes out through the hall.]*

MR. HARRISON, *showing* HENRY *the bottle:* Well, Henry, you old rascal! You think this'll hold him?

HENRY, *nodding:* Dat hol' mos' anybody, Mistah Harrison!

MR. HARRISON: Think we'll have enough food? Dr. Berkeley's mighty keen on Maggie's cooking.

HENRY: Yas, suh! 'Deed we will, suh.

MR. HARRISON: Well, if you have an extra bowl of gravy, I wouldn't mind seeing you drop it on Mr. Bingham.

HENRY, *laughing lightly:* Aw, go on, Mistah Harrison! You know I wouldn' do nothin' like dat. I always felt kind of sorry for Mistah Bingham, myse'f.

MR. HARRISON, *aghast:* Sorry for Mr. Bingham? Well, I'll be damned! If ever a soul on earth didn't want people to feel sorry for him, it's Jerry Bingham!

HENRY: Well, dat might be 'cause he tryin' not to feel sorry fo' his*se'f,* Mistah Harrison. Soon as other folks get to feelin' sorry fo' yo', yo' begins to feel sorry fo' yo'*se'f.* An' dat's de wuss thing can happen to yo'. Ain't *no*body bad enough off – no, nor good enough, either! – to start feelin' sorry fo' his*se'f.*

MR. HARRISON, *amazed:* Well, Henry, I declare! You're a philosopher, you are!

HENRY: 'Scuse me, suh? I's a which?

MR. HARRISON, *gesturing helplessly with the whiskey bottle:* You're a – er, one of those people who – well, they think, and they talk, and – well, it's hard to explain! But you're a philosopher, all right. A real philosopher! *[Picks up his newspaper from the floor and goes out through the hall to the livingroom.]*

HENRY, *scratching his head:* Well! Dat's de fus' time I ever see Mistah Harrison at a loss fo' words!

HENRY *turns to go out the door to the pantry.* JIM HARRISON *enters from the front hall. He is a young man of about nineteen and wears a black tuxedo without the coat. His bowtie hangs untied around his neck.*

JIM: Hey, Henry! Do me a favor! Tie this for me, will you? *[Points to his tie.]* I hate these damned things. Never have learned to tie one.

HENRY: Why, yas indeed, Mistah Jim. I'll be glad to. *[Begins tying the tie.]*

JIM: Thanks a lot. – Maggie did a great job on this shirt. I'd hate to wear a sloppy tie with it. Thank her for me, will you?

HENRY, *nodding:* I sho' will.

JIM: What was all the noise about down here? Sounded like Joshua at the battle of Jericho!

HENRY, *smiling:* Aw, I done hyared wuss, Mistah Jim.

JIM: Yeah, I guess so. You've been around here longer than I have.

HENRY: I didn' mean it dat way, Mistah Jim.

JIM: I know it! Just joking! But what was it this time? The old man's in-laws coming to visit?

HENRY, *finishing the tie:* Naw, suh – mo' like de *out*laws comin' dis time. Dr. Berkeley 'phoned he was bringin' Mistah Bingham wif him tonight an'–

JIM, *grinning:* Not old Jeremiah Bingham from Norfolk?

HENRY: Yas, suh! Dat's de one.

JIM: Well, I'll be damned! – That really ought to be good. I wish I didn't have to go to this dance tonight. Didn't want to anyway. It doesn't start till ten, though! *[Laughs.]* Old Bingham! He can't help stepping on people's toes. Too bad they have to be my father's! Bingham can really be funny.

HENRY: I don' b'lieve he be steppin' on toes tonight, Mistah Jim – 'ceptin' his own.

JIM: Why? What's happening?

HENRY: Well, yo' daddy done broke out some of his bes' whiskey, an' –

JIM, *annoyed: My dumb luck*! The very night I'm going out! Enough to make you wonder what the world's coming to!

HENRY, *smiling:* Mos' folks, when dey say dat, mean dey don' know what dey's comin' to dey*se'f*, Mistah Jim.

JIM: Well, its all these *little* things that go wrong – that's what gets me down. The big ones I don't mind so much: I'm ready for *them* to go wrong – half the time, anyway.

HENRY: Well, I guess you'd think I mus' done had a pretty good time of it, Mistah Jim. I ain't had nothin' but *big* troubles all *my* life.

JIM: Go on, Henry! You've had somebody looking after you since the day you were born.

HENRY, *nodding:* Yas, suh. But it's hard, sometimes, to figure out whether it's de Lawd or de Devil!

JIM, *laughing:* And have you finally figured it out?

HENRY: Well, not exac'ly. But I reckon if yo' *think* it was de Devil las' time an' *hope* it gonter be de Lawd de nex', yo' cain't go ver' far wrong. *[The doorbell rings as* HENRY *finishes.]*

JIM: Good grief! There they are and I haven't even got my coat on! *[Runs out through the hall and up the front stairs.]*

HENRY *goes back to the front door and opens it.* DR. BERKELEY *enters. He has a round, red face and is fat and prosperous-looking.*

DR. BERKELEY, *removing his hat and extending a hand to* HENRY: Henry! I haven't seen you in ages! *[They shake hands.]* You don't look a day older, though. How are you?

HENRY: Aw, pretty good, Dr. Berkeley.

DR. BERKELEY: Go on, Henry! God knows you're not good – and *I* know you're not pretty!

HENRY, *smiling but looking down at the floor:* I wisht I thought yo' was jokin', Dr. Berkeley.

DR. BERKELEY, *patting his shoulder affectionately:* For Pete's sake, Henry! Nobody does anything but joke with you! *[*MR. *and* MRS. HARRISON *enter the hall and come to the front door.]* Well, Helen, hello! How are you? And, George: you're looking healthy as ever, I'm sorry to say! *[He kisses* her *and shakes hands with* MR. HARRISON.*]*

MRS. HARRISON: John, I'm so glad to see you! But where is Jerry Bingham?

DR. BERKELEY: Oh, I told Jerry you expected him. He arrived a few minutes ago from Norfolk but said he couldn't impose on you. He told me *his* wife would never let *him* bring a friend home to dinner without any notice! Aren't some people silly?

DR. BERKELEY *turns and gives his hat and coat to* HENRY, *who carries them off left to the front-hall closet.* MRS. HARRISON *fixes her husband with a look of helpless disgust.*

MRS. HARRISON, *turning to* DR. BERKELEY: I'm *so* sorry! We were all looking forward to seeing him.

MR. HARRISON, *doubting his luck:* You mean he isn't coming at *all*?

MRS. HARRISON, *jabbing him in the ribs with an elbow as she leads* DR. BERKELEY *off left to the livingroom*: George is *so* disappointed. – Tell me, John: what have you heard from your sister in California? *[They both go off talking, as* HENRY *comes back into the diningroom.]*

MR. HARRISON, *grinning at* HENRY: Well, I'll be damned! *[Follows his wife and* DR. BERKELEY *off left.]*

HENRY *smiles faintly, then sighs, and begins picking up the extra silverware from the table. Suddenly he drops the silver with a clatter and clutches his chest. He coughs violently, doubles over, and catches at one of the chairs.*

The pantry door opens: MAGGIE, *the Negro cook, appears. She is much younger than* HENRY *and has an open face with large, brown eyes.*

MAGGIE, *entering cautiously:* Henry! Henry! What's de matter, Henry?

HENRY, *not looking at her, but breathing hard and still holding on to the chair:* No mind 'bout me, Maggie! – Nothin' – ain't nothin' wrong! – I gon' be all right.

MAGGIE, *frightened:* You *sick,* Henry! I gon' call Miz Harrison right now! *[Starts across to the hall doorway.]*

HENRY, *straightening himself and speaking firmly:* Naw, *don't* yo', Maggie! *[Terrified,* MAGGIE *stops where she is.* HENRY *still leans heavily on the chair.]* Maggie! Maggie, tell me – does yo' 'member what I ask yo' 'bout – yestiddy? – Does yo' 'member dat – Maggie?

MAGGIE, *still frightened:* Yas, Henry! I 'member 'bout it.

HENRY: Does yo' 'member what – what yo' promised yo'd do?

MAGGIE: Yas, Henry! But don' think 'bout dat –

HENRY, *breathing a little easier:* Naw, I ain't got long to think 'bout it, Maggie. – I want to make sho' yo' hadn' forgot'. – Yo' won't – yo' won't fail me – will yo', Maggie?

MAGGIE, *coming forward timidly and placing her hand on* HENRY'S *arm:* Naw, Henry. I promise yo' I won't. But you sick! Lemme go call Miz Harrison!

HENRY, *not looking at her, but putting his hand on top of hers:* Naw – I gon' be all right, Maggie. – In jes' a little while – I gon' be all right!

The stage darkens to denote the passage of approximately two hours.

When the curtain rises again, MR. *and* MRS. HARRISON, DR. BERKELEY, *and* JIM *are seated around the diningroom table. They have just finished dessert.* HENRY *is clearing the table.*

DR. BERKELEY: Well, that was a wonderful dinner. Henry, you and Maggie haven't lost a bit of your old skill.

HENRY, *as he removes the dessert platter:* I'll tell Maggie yo' enjoyed it, suh! *[Goes out pantry door with the platter.]*

MRS. HARRISON: You think it'll hold you till *you* learn to cook like that, John?

DR. BERKELEY: I wish I had faith enough to think so!

MR. HARRISON: To think what? – that the dinner will hold you?

DR. BERKELEY: No! – that I'll ever be able to cook that way. *[*MR. HARRISON *laughs.]*

MRS. HARRISON: Well, Henry has faith enough to spare. You ought to borrow some of his.

DR. BERKELEY: Oh, but Henry's faith is a different kind.

MRS. HARRISON: That's why I told you to borrow some.

MR. HARRISON: If John took enough to do *him* any good, Henry wouldn't have any left. *[*DR. BERKELEY *chuckles.]*

JIM: Even so, I think Henry would give it to you!

DR. BERKELEY, *becoming serious:* I think you're right, Jim.

MR. HARRISON: Well, I envy Henry's faith, myself. I bet he's happier than any of us.

DR. BERKELEY: I envy even more his willingness to share it. If *I* had that much faith, I don't believe I'd part with one small ounce of it!

JIM: I think every one has about the same capacity for belief. But to put your faith in God, you have to cut down on what you put elsewhere.

MR. HARRISON: That would explain your trouble, John. You've too much faith in yourself.

MRS. HARRISON: George! You'll spoil John's evening. *He* always thought it was because he had too much sense!

DR. BERKELEY, *laughing:* Well, what's the difference? [HENRY *comes back in from the pantry.]* Henry, come to my rescue! They're saying bad things about me!

HENRY, *smiling:* Cain't nobody say bad things 'bout yo' 'cept yo'*se'f*, Dr. Berkeley. Nobody else know de half of it!

DR. BERKELEY, *laughing:* How about the Lord, Henry? Doesn't *he* know?

HENRY, *looking serious:* Yas, suh, but de Lawd don' cuss yo' in *front* o' nobody. It's jes' you an' him when *he* git to talkin'.

DR. BERKELEY: Do you honestly believe the Lord is going to speak to you?

HENRY: Not jes' to me, Dr. Berkeley. He gonter have it out wif *ever'*body 'fo' he finish. Ever' dog gonter have his day!

DR. BERKELEY: And man is like a dog, eh, Henry? Sufficient unto his evil is the day thereof! *[Laughs, as* HENRY *looks puzzled.]* Well, has the Lord been to see *you* any time recently?

HENRY: Naw, suh. I reckon he got better things to do. But I 'spec' he'll git 'roun' to me 'fo' long. My daddy use' to tell me dat, if yo' is alive, it mean de Lawd was dere when yo' was born – an' 'fo' yo' can die, de Lawd have to be dere, too – jes' to let yo' know it's all right wif him.

JIM: Well, Henry, you're not ready to die!

HENRY, *shaking his head:* Not 'less de Lawd say so, Mistah Jim. I ain't good enough yet, so I kind o' scared to see him. He don't come fo' yo' 'less he think' you's good enough to go 'way wif him – or 'less he think' you's had enough time an' yo' ain't gonter get no better.

MR. HARRISON: Henry, you amaze me! But if being a good butler has anything to do with it, I think you're safe enough.

DR. BERKELEY: I'll say a good word for you, too, Henry. You mix the best Old Fashioned I ever tasted!

HENRY, *talking as if to himself:* I'm 'fraid dat won't do me no good, Dr. Berkeley. – Won't do me no good at all. *[Puts his hand up to his heart.]* Won't do me no good –

As HENRY *speaks, the four at the table freeze in their respective attitudes.* HENRY *looks up suddenly to see the figure of a man standing across the room from him. The figure is a tall, dignified Negro with snow-white hair. He wears a black suit with long frock coat, spotless white shirt, and string bowtie. He looks like an ancient country preacher. He stands and smiles at* HENRY, *who stares back at him blankly.*

FIGURE, *speaking slowly:* Henry Hill! – Henry Hill! – How yo' makin' out, Henry?

HENRY, *frightened:* Who talkin' to me like dat? How you git in hyar?

FIGURE: I jes' walked in, Henry – same as you. Been a long time since you come to see me. I figured maybe I better come see *you.*

HENRY, *starting to tremble:* Couldn' nobody but de Lawd be tellin' me dat!

FIGURE: An' couldn' nobody but Henry Hill be dat scared to see me!

HENRY: Aw, Lawd, I was 'fraid you'd come tonight! – 'fo' I was ready! I knew it, Lawd! I knew it!

FIGURE: What yo' mean, Henry –"'fo' you was ready"? Yo' done *had* close to sebenty years. Yo' still ain't ready, after all dat time?

HENRY: Lawd, I been tryin' – 'deed I have! But it take' a long time, Lawd – mighty long time, fo' a man like me. I – I prob'ly couldn' do it in a hunnert years, Lawd!

FIGURE: Well, maybe it's good I come when I did. Maybe you wastin' my time – an' your'n, too.

HENRY, *shaking his head:* Aw, naw, I – I didn' mean it like dat, Lawd! I mean, I'd keep on tryin', but – but it still gonter be mighty hard!

FIGURE: Well, a hunnert years is a long time, Henry. So's sebenty years, too. In all dat time a man's liable to forgit 'bout what he's doin' – or what he's already done.

HENRY, *trembling:* Aw, naw, Lawd, I ain't forgot'! I ain't never forgot'!

FIGURE, *slowly, emphatically:* But is yo' sure yo' ain't never tried, Henry? Is yo' sure yo' ain't never *tried?*

HENRY *puts his hands up to his eyes. The figure disappears. Suddenly the four at the table come once more to life with general laughter.* HENRY, *startled, drops his hands from his eyes. He looks wildly about for an instant, then recollects himself.*

DR. BERKELEY, *laughing heartily:* Well, Henry, you old sinner! I bet you and the Lord'll get along famously! You know, he never has spoken to *me*!

MR. HARRISON: You've never spoken to *him*, John! Or maybe you've forgotten to try! *[All at the table laugh.]*

HENRY, *breathing heavily as he moves his hand across his chest:* Naw, Lawd, I ain't forgot'!

MR. HARRISON: What's that, Henry?

HENRY, *looking round quickly from the spot where the figure had stood:* Nothin'! Nothin', suh! 'Scuse me, Miz Harrison, did yo' want anything else, ma'am?

MRS. HARRISON: Some coffee, please, Henry.

HENRY: Yas, ma'am. *[Picks up a silver tray from the sideboard and places her cup and saucer on it.]*

DR. BERKELEY: I'd like some, too, while you're at it, Henry. You really make fine coffee. I'll mention that instead of the Old Fashioned, if you'd like!

HENRY: Yas, suh. *[Places* DR. BERKELEY'S *cup on the tray and goes out to the pantry.]*

MRS. HARRISON: Really, John! You two shouldn't tease Henry so. He feels his religion very deeply.

DR. BERKELEY, *nodding good-naturedly:* I know, Helen. I wouldn't tease him if he didn't!

MRS. HARRISON: I'm serious, John! His father was a preacher, you know – a grand-looking old man. Luther Hill was his name. He must have been six and a half feet tall, with perfectly white hair. His brother was my mother's chauffeur for years. Mother used to send their family presents every Christmas. Our visit to Luther's little house on Christmas Eve was always one of the happiest times of the whole season.

DR. BERKELEY: I had no idea! – Henry himself wouldn't cut a bad figure as a preacher, you know.

MRS. HARRISON, *nodding:* Henry's very much like his father. Luther Hill used to tell my mother how proud he was going to be when Henry took over the congregation. But Henry never seemed to want it. He left home and worked on his own for a while – joined the army during the First World War. He came to us after he was discharged. – But even now he acts so much like his father sometimes, that I think I'm seeing a ghost!

JIM, *nodding:* Many a time he's preached at me! – And I think the Bible is the only book he ever reads.

DR. BERKELEY: Well, they say there's an awful lot in it! *[They all laugh lightly.]*

MR. HARRISON: Ah, this *has* been a most enjoyable dinner! I never dreamed it would be so pleasant.

DR. BERKELEY: We have your gracious wife to thank for that, George. Why, if I ever found some one who'd treat me *half* as nicely, I might get married myself.

MRS. HARRISON: Why, John Berkeley! You wouldn't get married if your life depended on it!

DR. BERKELEY: I'm not so sure! Of course, I'm thankful my life never *has* depended on it, but –!

MR. HARRISON *bursts out laughing, then checks himself abruptly.*

MRS. HARRISON: I feel quite complimented, John. I'm sure it's years since you even *thought* about getting married!

DR. BERKELEY, *nodding:* Sixty-one, my next birthday. – It's just as well: no one would have thought about it with me.

JIM: Women aren't *that* hard to get along with, are they, Dr. Berkeley?

DR. BERKELEY: Well, if you *think* so when you're young, you'll believe it by the time you're my age. – If you want to get married, Jim, just don't think about it. Just don't think, *period.* Then, when you're hitched, you won't *mind* not thinking when your wife wants to do it for you.

MR. HARRISON: Good God, John! *[As this speech begins,* HENRY *comes back from the pantry with the two cups of coffee. He serves them carefully to* MRS. HARRISON *and* DR. BERKELEY.*]* I don't want my son going off to a party with talk like *that* in his head. How about it, Henry? Can't *you* say something to reflect a bit better on bachelors?

DR. BERKELEY: That's right! You never got married, either, did you, Henry?

JIM: Well, why *didn't* you get married, Henry? I've never heard you on that subject.

MAGGIE, *appearing at the pantry door, frightened:* M-Miz Harrison! 'Scuse me, ma'am! *[They all turn to look at her except* HENRY, *who stares down at the floor.]*

HENRY: Aw, I – I don' know, Mistah Jim. I jes' – I jes' never had de time, I reckon!

MAGGIE: Miz Harrison, Henry's sick! Dey's somethin' wrong wif him!

Again, the four at the table – together with MAGGIE – *freeze in their positions. The figure in black appears across the room as before. He glares at* HENRY, *who cannot lift his eyes from the floor.*

FIGURE, *beginning calmly but speaking with passion as he goes on:* Why didn' yo' tell dat boy de truth, Henry? Why didn' yo' tell him de *truth*? Yo' knows yo' was fixing' to marry dat gal down yonder in Georgia. Yo' knows it, don't yo'?

HENRY: Aw, Lawd, I –!

FIGURE: Well, what's de matter? Have yo' forgot' 'bout it? Answer me, Henry. Have yo' forgot' 'bout it 'cause it was *forty years ago?*

HENRY: Naw, Lawd, I ain't forgot!

FIGURE: Tell me right, Henry. Have yo' forgot' 'bout runnin' 'way from home to marry a gal yo' didn' hardly know? – an' de only reason yo' wanted her was dat she happen' to be *goodlookin'*? Have yo' forgot' 'bout findin' her in de house wif a white man when yo' got dere?

HENRY: *trembling:* Naw, Lawd!

FIGURE: Have yo' forgot' what happen when yo' found 'em, Henry? Have yo' forgot' 'bout beatin' de man's head till dere warn't nothin' lef' to beat? – An' do yo' remember what yo' did to de *gal?* Tell me *dat*, Henry! Do yo' remember how she scream'? Can yo' see her now de way she look' when yo' choked her? Do yo' *remember* dat, Henry?

HENRY: Aw, Lawd, I ain't no mo' 'n jes' a man! *[Puts his hands up over his face.]*

FIGURE: Yo' mean yo' didn' *try* to be no mo' 'n jes' a man, don't yo', Henry? – Do yo' remember her mother and her father, old and helpless like dey was? And she de only chile, de woman yo' was fixin' to marry! An' do yo' remember –after yo'd got yo'se'f in de army to git 'way from de law – do yo' remember dat man yo' could o' saved by carryin' him thirty yards wif yo', but yo' lef' him to die 'cause he was *white?* – Have yo' forgot' 'bout all dat, Henry, 'cause it been so long ago? *Have* yo', Henry?

HENRY, *falling to his knees and crying out:* Naw, Lawd, I 'members it! I ain't never forgot'! I 'members it all!

FIGURE, *slowly and deliberately:* Well, I'm glad yo' do, Henry. I'm glad yo' remembers all dat. – Cause *I* remembers it, too!

The figure disappears. HENRY *clutches his chest and breathes in gasps. The four at the table come alive at once.* MAGGIE *remains at the pantry door.* MRS. HARRISON, *seeing* HENRY *on his knees, gets up and goes to him.* DR. BERKELEY *follows her. The others rise in their places.*

MRS. HARRISON: John! Do something! I think it's his heart! He had an attack last week.

HENRY *struggles to rise.* DR. BERKELEY *helps him.*

DR. BERKELEY: What's the matter, Henry? Where's the pain?

HENRY, *crying out:* It's cuttin' into my soul! Lawd, let me forgit! *[Collapses in* DR. BERKELEY'S *arms.]*

MR. HARRISON: Can I get you anything, John?

DR. BERKELEY, *laying* HENRY *down on the floor:* No, not a thing. *[Feels* HENRY'S *pulse and then his heart.]*

MAGGIE, *coming forward timidly:* Yo' don' mean he dead, does yo', Dr. Berkeley?

DR. BERKELEY: I'm afraid so, Maggie. But he wasn't in pain for long. God certainly answered that last prayer!

JIM: Henry dead? He can't be! We were joking with him a moment ago!

DR. BERKELEY, *shaking his head:* Poor old fellow! – Didn't you tell me he'd never been to a doctor, George?

MR. HARRISON, *nodding:* I did! In all his years with us he never had the slightest thing wrong with him – until last week.

DR. BERKELEY: That's odd. I would have sworn I felt something on his back. Did he wear any sort of orthopedic brace?

MR. HARRISON: Why, no – I never knew of anything like that.

DR. BERKELEY, *stooping and running his hand under* HENRY'S *back:* He *does* have something there! *[Moves his hand across* HENRY'S *chest.]* I can feel it on his chest, too! *[Glances up at* MR. *and* MRS. HARRISON, *who stare back, surprised.]* I'll just have a look at this. *[Reaches to loosen* HENRY's *tie.]*

MAGGIE *has been watching anxiously. Now she runs forward, kneels beside* HENRY *and places her hands over* DR. BERKELEY'S.

MAGGIE, *pleading:* Naw, suh, Dr. Berkeley! Don' bother him, suh! He tol' me yestiddy mornin' he want to be buried jes' de way he die'. Yas, suh, he did! *[Pulls an old leather purse out of the bosom of her dress and shows it to* DR. BERKELEY.*]* He gave me dis money to see him buried wif – tol' me where he want' to be put. He say he knew he warn't good enough to deserve no fun'ral. He jes' want' to be buried soon as he die'. He say he want' to go in de ground in jes' what he have on – didn' want nobody botherin' wif his clothes nor nothin'!

DR. BERKELEY: There, there, Maggie. I'm just going to open his shirt. It's nothing to be upset about.

MAGGIE: Aw, naw, suh, Doctor! Please, let him be! Don' bother him none! *[Turns desperately to* MR. HARRISON.*]* Mistah Harrison, suh! He look' at me like he was dead already, when he say it! An' I was scared, jes' like I am now! *Please* let me take care of him, suh! Don' bother him none! I promised Henry I wouldn' let nothin' happen to him, suh. I promised him 'fo' he die'! *[Breaks off in tears.]* Let me take care of him de way he want'! He give me de money, an' I tol' him I would, Mistah Harrison!

MR. HARRISON *goes to* MAGGIE, *raises her from her knees, and puts his arm around her shoulders.*

MR. HARRISON: Now, Maggie, don't trouble yourself. Of course, we're going to give Henry the best burial we can. I'll take care of all that – don't worry. But we won't be able to have the funeral for a day or two. I'll have to get him some clothes to be buried in. Henry never bought him*self* a new suit in his life! I'll take care of everything. You keep your money. Don't worry yourself! *[Gently pushes her hand and the little purse back toward* MAGGIE.*]*

MAGGIE: Naw, suh, dat ain't my money, Mistah Harrison. Dat's Henry's money. Dat's all he ever save' fo' hisse'f, 'cause I seed him send mos' of it off ever' week to somewhar in Georgia. Ever' week till jes' a few years ago. Dat ain't my money, Mistah Harrison. Dat's Henry's own buryin' money. Please, suh, don' bother wif no fun'ral nor nothin'. Jes' let me bury him like he want. *[Begins crying again.]* He want' to go in de ground jes' like he was! – jes' like he was!

MR. HARRISON, *thoughtfully:* I never knew he had any family in Georgia.

MRS. HARRISON, *going to* MAGGIE: Maggie, don't cry! Somebody's going to have to get him ready for the funeral. Henry won't know anything about it.

MAGGIE, *sobbing:* But Henry don' want no fun'ral, Miz Harrison! Please, don' let nobody bother him!

MR. HARRISON *goes to* HENRY *and stoops over him with* DR. BERKELEY.

MRS. HARRISON, *tenderly, as she takes* MAGGIE *in her arms:* We won't do anything Henry would mind, Maggie. Now, now, don't upset yourself!

MAGGIE, *seeing the two men start to unbutton* HENRY'S shirt, *goes to* HENRY *and kneels beside him, clutching* MR. HARRISON'S *hands in hers.*

MAGGIE: Naw, suh! Please, don' bother him, suh! Please, don' bother him! I promised an' I's scared, Mistah Harrison! Henry was a good man, an' if he don' want nobody after him when he die', he have a reason, suh. I *know* he do! I's scared, Mistah Harrison! I's scared!

The two men stop unbuttoning the shirt and look at each other. They turn toward MAGGIE, *who is sobbing uncontrollably.* MR. HARRISON *at length gets up and takes* MAGGIE *by the hand back to* MRS. HARRISON. *The two of them try in vain to comfort her.* MAGGIE *does not stop crying. She continues to sob quietly through the rest of the scene.*

JIM, *who has been standing to one side, watching, now goes to his father.*

JIM: Dad, if Maggie feels this way, maybe we'd better let *her* take care of Henry. After all, he did ask her and she promised before he died –

MRS. HARRISON: Perhaps he's right, George. If Henry wanted it that way, it's the least we can do.

MR. HARRISON: Oh, I'm sure it's nothing serious! Maggie's over-wrought by the suddenness of it. Of course, I'm going to do what's right by Henry!

DR. BERKELEY *meanwhile, after glancing at the others as they argue, has turned back to* HENRY *and begun to unbutton the shirt. He continues until he can see what lies beneath it. He lifts the cloth and stares unbelievingly. He opens his mouth as if to speak but says nothing. Then he pulls the shirt together and remains kneeling, his eyes fixed on* HENRY'S chest.

MR. HARRISON *suddenly notices that his wife is staring at the doctor.* MR. HARRISON *turns, looks at* DR. BERKELEY, *and moves toward him uneasily.* MRS. HARRISON *watches, her arms still around* MAGGIE. *The doctor gets up as* MR. HARRISON *approaches.*

MR. HARRISON: What's the matter, John? Is something wrong?

DR. BERKELEY *continues to stare at* HENRY.

MR. HARRISON, *putting his hand on* DR. BERKELEY'S *arm*: John, what's the matter? What *is* it?

DR. BERKELEY, *as if dazed:* A chain!

MR. HARRISON, *dropping his hand:* What?

DR. BERKELEY, *without looking at him:* A chain! A heavy chain! – 'Round and 'round his chest, like a snake!

MR. HARRISON: What the devil – !

MR. HARRISON *turns and is about to stoop and look at the body.* DR. BERKELEY *grasps his arm, never taking his eyes off* HENRY.

DR. BERKELEY: It's eaten into his *flesh*! Almost embedded in places. – Must have worn the thing for years.

MR. HARRISON: Good God! Is it possible?

DR. BERKELEY, *dropping the other's arm:* For *years*! I would have killed myself first! He must have worn it for *years*!

MR. HARRISON: But it's absurd! Why on earth would he do such a thing? It's not human – it's not possible – it's –

DR. BERKELEY, *turning on* MR. HARRISON: *Look*, then, you fool, if you don't believe it's possible! *Look! I* thought it was a chain, but *I* couldn't believe it! That's why *I* looked. *[Turns back to* HENRY *and speaks more softly.]* If that old man wore chains, what are you and I to wear? *[Continues staring at* HENRY'S *chest.]*

MR. HARRISON *looks first at the dead man and then away at the floor. At last he turns and walks back to* MAGGIE, *who is hiding her face in her hands.*

MR. HARRISON: I'm sorry, Maggie! You were right.

Only the sound of MAGGIE *weeping softly into her hands is heard as the curtain falls.*